D1003456

MOUNTAINMAN
CRAFTS AND SKILLS

MOUNTAINMAN
CRAFTS AND SKILLS

A FULLY ILLUSTRATED GUIDE TO WILDERNESS LIVING AND SURVIVAL

by
David R. Montgomery

THE LYONS PRESS

Printed in Canada

Originally published in 1992 by Horizon Publishers

10 9 8 7 6 5 4 3 2 1

Library of Congress Cataloging-in-Publication Data

Montgomery, David R.
    Mountainman crafts and skills: a fully illustrated guide to
wilderness living and survival / by David R. Montgomery.
        p. cm.
    Originally published: Bountiful, Utah : Horizon Publishers, c1980.
    Includes bibliographical references and index.
    ISBN 1-58574-066-7 (pbk.)
    1. Handicraft—West (U.S.) 2. Trappers—West (U.S.)—Social life
and customs—19th century. 3. Wilderness survival—West (U.S.)—
Equipment and supplies. 4. West (U.S.)—Social life and customs—
19th century. I. Title.

TT23.6 .M65 2000
796.5—dc21   CIP
                                                        00-021623

Contents

1

Mountain Man Tools and Materials

The Work Area

Since the Mountain Man spent the greater portion of his time outdoors, his skills and crafts were utilized in the open—on the ground, on a log, etc. This work environment could naturally be utilized today as well, and it is by far the cheapest area to work in. A garage with a workbench, or an extra room in the house, could be used as a work area. A tipi pitched in the backyard could also be used for the messier jobs such as tanning. Through the community schools program, school facilities in the shop or craft areas occasionally can be utilized.

The best situation is to have an area where you can have a workbench, electricity, storage area, and a place to hang the hides you are working on. You may be able to go the extra mile and build an area specifically for your mountain man crafts.

Tools and Equipment

Most of the tools used by a mountain man were what he could carry with him as he trapped. They consisted of sometimes both a Dadely and a Greenriver butcher knife, a steel or bone awl, a throwing ax, a patch knife, traps, flint and steel, and of course a black powder rifle, as well as a bullet mold. With these basic tools he could survive quite comfortably in the wilderness. For extended crafts in this area, though, more tools and equipment would help. The following is quite an extensive list, not all of which are absolutely necessary.

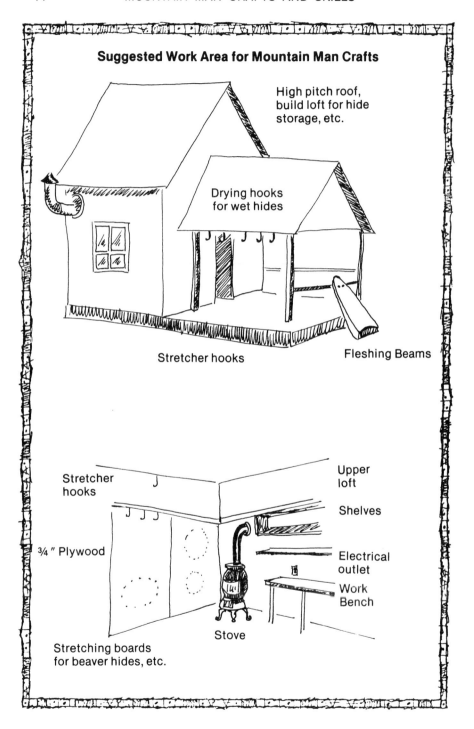

Suggested Work Area for Mountain Man Crafts

High pitch roof, build loft for hide storage, etc.

Drying hooks for wet hides

Stretcher hooks

Fleshing Beams

Stretcher hooks

Upper loft

Shelves

¾ " Plywood

Electrical outlet

Work Bench

Stove

Stretching boards for beaver hides, etc.

Most of these tools can be found in the home, and some of the equipment can be made at home. Even an inexperienced person can make a simple pulling stake and slicker. It is up to each individual how much he or she wants to spend. The decision depends greatly on what items are already on hand.

A pulling bench can be made out of scrap wood, threaded pipe, some bolts, and an old used saw blade for less than $10. If you have a 2″ × 4″ × 2′ board sharpened on one end and a good bench vise it will cost nothing. Paddles can be made from a 1″ × 4″, cutting it to shape with a hand saw. A fleshing beam can be made from an old wooden ironing board if one can be found (that's what I use— a 1936 model as a matter of fact), or any type of wood put together to form a big enough area to flesh a deer hide.

Five gallon plastic buckets used for mud in dry walling can usually be obtained from a construction site when builders are working on the interiors. They can also be obtained from some grocery store bakeries.

Tools such as drills, bits, whetstones, buffers, bench grinders, hammers, saws, tape measures, vises, and dremel tools can be purchased at local hardware stores.

Awls with automatic stitching can be purchased at leather craft stores as well as leather punches with a cost of from $3.00 to $5.00. Glover needles may be found at saddle shops or shoe repair shops. Sail mending needles can be found at sailboat shops and sometimes at Black Powder shops that sell the works.

Engraving tools can be obtained at good art supply stores.

Trapping supplies can be purchased in most states. Some of the larger suppliers for traps, trapping books, and scents are:

Woodstream Corp., Lititz, Pa., 17543
Necina Fur Co., Box 787, Jamestown, Ohio, 45335

Prices as of this writing are about $2.40 for #110 conibear, $2.80 for #1 Stop Loss Long Spring, $12.00 for #330 conibear, and $6.50 for #4 Long Springs.

Gathering tools and supplies is up to the individual, and is affected by the amount he wants to spend and how long he wants to spend looking for the items. Gathering these things gradually has worked best for me, although it has taken a couple of years to do so, and it has been worth it. Your finished projects will please you for a lifetime.

Tanning Tools

pulling bench - not essential, but nice to have. Used to shave and stretch hides, i.e., deer, antelope, beaver, muskrat
pulling stake - important for stretching hides in the tanning process
slicker or paddle - the hair and epidermus must be removed with this instrument when doing hides with hair off
draw knife - a butcher knife can be used in its place to remove meat and fat from hide
fleshing beam - a beam used to lay the hide over to flesh it
two 20-gallon plastic or wooden barrels - these containers are for tanning solutions
two 5-gallon plastic containers - these smaller containers are for tanning muskrat, rabbit, etc.
whetstone and steel - needed for sharpening knives
skinning knife - used for skinning game
rags - essential for keeping tools clean

Clothing-Making Tools

awl - used for punching holes in leather for sewing
glover's needle - sharpened needle which can sew through thin leather
sail mending needle - sharpened curved needle which can be used with sinew to sew through leather
beading needles - various types to use in decorating clothing
rope - used for hanging up and tousing tanned hides on

Tools for General Craft Work

drill and bits - for riflemaking, horn work, etc.
buffer - polishing horn, knives, etc.
vise - for holding horn, rifle parts, and drilling
hammer - general purpose
screw driver - rifle building
plane - rifle building
tape measure - clothing, rifle and horn use
straight edge - drawing straight lines on patterns
files - filing rifle, horns, etc.
bottles of various sizes - storing beads, quills, buttons
brushes of various sizes - for painting tipi, willow chairs, etc.
dremel tool - great for grinding small areas on rifles and horns

engraving tools - useful if any designs are going to be engraved into the barrel

hot plate - melting wax, heating water to soften cow horn

stool - to sit on

Traps

wire

pliers

#1 Long Spring Stop-Loss (Victor or B&L) - for muskrat

#330 Conibear - for beaver

#4 Long Spring - for beaver

#110 Conibear - for muskrat

Tools for Tanning Hides

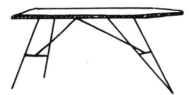

Old Wooden
Ironing Board
can be used for
a fleshing beam

   or   

Wooden Barrel   or   Plastic Barrel

Draw Knife
without teeth
used
for
slicker

Draw Knife
with teeth
for
fleshing

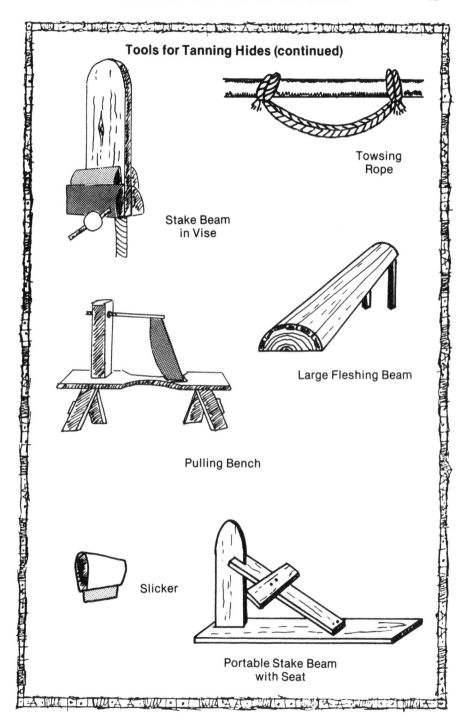

Tools for Tanning Hides (continued)

Towsing Rope

Stake Beam in Vise

Large Fleshing Beam

Pulling Bench

Slicker

Portable Stake Beam with Seat

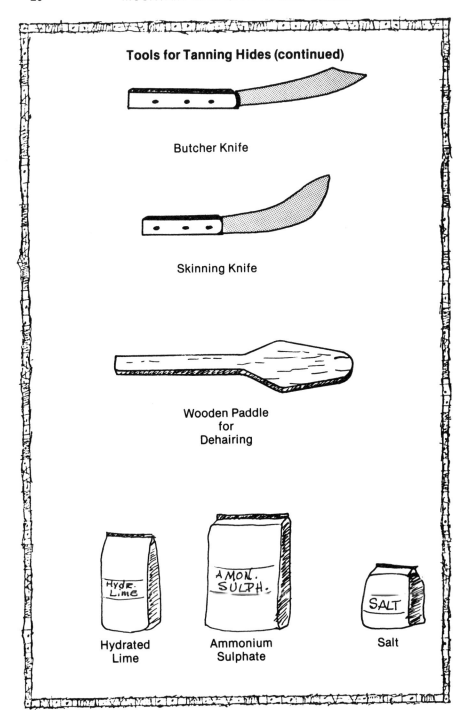

Tools for Tanning Hides (continued)

Butcher Knife

Skinning Knife

Wooden Paddle
for
Dehairing

Hydrated
Lime

Ammonium
Sulphate

Salt

2

Traps
and
Trappings

Civilization ended at St. Louis in the early 1800's. It was there that the mountain men would outfit themselves with horses, food, and trapping gear. Ten traps were generally enough to work with, but extras were needed because the traps would often end up being lost, stolen by Indians, or carried away by a sly animal. Leg traps were the only type used at that time, although other types are available now.

There were several reasons why trapping on a large scale came about. The demand for beaver pelts to make beaver felt hats for the fashionable people of Europe was perhaps the major reason. Contributing factors were the desire of governments for exploration and acquisition of new territories, and the desire on the part of adventurous individuals to get away from civilization.

The skill of trapping today can benefit you in various ways. There may come a time when you need to survive on what you can catch for food and clothing. Extra income can be had from trapping muskrat, fox and coyote. You may want to store furs and hides for future use, or you may want to make your own mountain man paraphernalia. It must be noted that you may live in an area where trapping can be done, so before you purchase your traps, it would be wise to check out the area first.

Types of Traps

There are three types of traps commonly used for beaver and muskrat trapping. The Conibear kills instantly and the leg traps require proper setting for drowning purposes. The preceeding chapter gives information concerning price and where to purchase.

Conibear

Victor Leg Trap

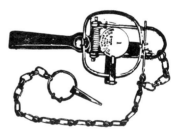

Stop-Loss Trap

Setting Your Traps

To begin with, it is a good idea to set your traps before you go out in the cold water and get your fingers caught. It could be a very painful experience otherwise. To set the *conibear*, squeeze the single spring with both hands, on top of your leg. Then, still holding

tight with one hand, use the other to take the body grips and pull them in the opposite direction of each other until the ends meet. While holding the body grips together, let go of the spring. It will stay as it is as long as the grips are held together. Now set the notched latch in the notch holding the trip wire and the spring. Gently let go with the other hand and the latch should hold.

The *leg-hold* trap has two types of leg catches on each trap. They are the jaws that clamp the foot and a wire that springs over the leg or shoulder to prevent the animal from reaching its leg to chew it off. Push the leaf spring down, using your leg or stump to brace the trap, making sure the pan is still under the jaws and the latch is not. Pull the spring wire over the jaws, then hold that and the leaf spring down together with one hand while pulling the jaws apart with the other. When the jaws are pushed down, it will keep both springs down. Now set the latch over the jaw and under the notch of the pan. It is best to do this part by reaching underneath with your fingers and setting it, in case you lose hold with your other hand and catch your fingers. Gently ease up on the jaws until the jaw pushes against the latch. If you see that it will hold, let go of the jaws and the trap is set.

There are six good basic methods for setting traps for muskrat and beaver in the following pages, and I've had good results with them.

Trapping Muskrat

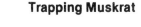

Streams, irrigation canals, swamps, rivers, ponds, and lakes are likely spots for muskrat. Pelts are prime only in the winter. Each state has its own regulations regarding the taking of fur bearers and it would be wise to check with your Wildlife Division before you do any trapping. Use the Conibear and Stop-Loss traps only—this will insure that the muskrat won't chew his leg off and escape.

What signs should you look for? Watch for areas on the bank that have been scratched or dug right at water level. Also holes (at least as big as a man's fist) at water level or just below, and logs or stumps that have animal droppings on them. Be on the lookout for scent piles—little mounds of mud or a sand bar with a great amount of oval droppings where the muskrat will normally come to pay a nightly visit.

Upon finding a scent mound, take two stop-loss traps and set them in the two most likely spots where the muskrat will climb upon

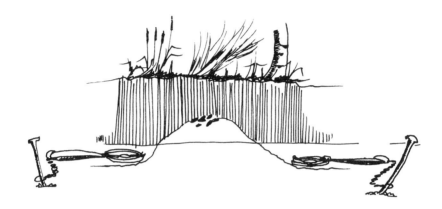

the mound. If the traps are set in the water, they must be at least an inch under water or the trap will freeze up. You could build a nest of weeds to put underneath the traps to keep them above water. As long as they don't get wet they won't freeze. Stake the chain out into deep water as far as possible, since the muskrat will swim for deep water and drown. A drowning stick is also helpful. This is placed out just far enough for the muskrat to swim around it and get tangled up and drown. This is especially good in shallow water.

You can tell if a bank hole is being used by the residue of twigs, vegetation, and the lack of cobwebs in it. If it is deep and at water line, set a conibear at the hole with only the latch above water. It can be set down on the bottom or on a weed bed to set it up higher. Put a forked stick in the spring to keep it from being knocked over.

Since muskrat are vegetarian, they seek roots and soft bark. You will notice where a pocket is being dug in bank. Set a trap out about four inches from the spot on a nest or directly on the bottom of the creek, pond, or river. Take a piece of carrot or apple and put it on a stick and stick it in the pocket above the water.

If there are logs or stumps on the water's edge, check them for droppings. If there are no signs there, don't bother to set a trap unless you have plenty to spare. If signs are present, set a carrot on the log or stump in such a way that the muskrat will have to step into the trap to get the bait. If the log or stump is small enough, you can wire the trap chain right to it.

These three methods will give you a high percentage catch as long as muskrats are active in the area. If the terrain has a high

population of muskrats, check your traps as early as possible in the morning. Other muskrats will sometimes bite the trapped one, which doesn't enhance the value of the hide.

Trapping Beaver

The two types of traps used for beaver are the conibear and the #4 leg trap.

Conibear   **#4 Leg Trap**

Beaver are found across most of the United States. The Rocky Mountain area has a larger amount of beaver than other areas. They live around or in streams, poonds, lakes and rivers where there is an abundance of aspen, cottonwood, and willows. If you find trees with large sections chewed, or downed trees, or willow brush that is cut near the base, you are most likely in beaver country. More sure signs are beaver lodges, dams with freshly-peeled sticks, and large holes in river banks at the water line.

Beaver trapping is becoming more profitable and it is a great sport. An individual can find many uses for beaver hides such as making hats, leggings, gloves, collars, blankets, capes, and decorative wall hangings.

If leg traps are to be used, always make sure the trap is weighted enough to drown the beaver when it swims to deeper water. A heavy rock or piece of steel can be wired to the trap.

Beaver meat is edible and is rich tasting. Clean it out, boil it in salt water and tenderize with papaya juice or other natural tenderizers, then bake it. Beaver in the Eastern states are now being trapped for their meat as well as pelts. Beaver tail, regardless of how good the mountain men of old said it was, isn't that good. It's nothing more than fat with two small strips of meat down each side of the tail bone.

Only muskrat and beaver trapping have been explained here because it is mainly beaver that the mountain man trapped. If you are interested in trapping other animals, a magazine called *Fur-Fish-Game* has a large section of ads concerning books on trapping. It is also an excellent trapping magazine in itself. It's cost is $.75 an issue and the address is:

Fur-Fish-Game
2878 E. Main Street
Columbus, Ohio 43209
Phone 614-231-9585

Follow the basic trapping methods explained here and you'll have a good, successful experience.

Beaver Dam Set

Conibear Trap

It is now always necessary to bait the beaver. When doing a dam set, the beaver will come to repair the dam if it is an active pond.

The conibear is best used on a dam set when the pond is too small for a leg hold trap.

1. Knock out a foot-wide section of the dam.

2. Set the conibear in place and stake each spring down, then wire to another stake. Make the trap secure so it won't get knocked over.

Beaver Dam Set

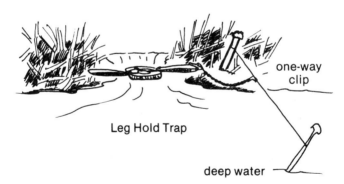

one-way clip

Leg Hold Trap

deep water

The leg hold is a favorable trap to use when there is deep water and larger ponds.

1. Knock a one-foot hole in the dam.

2. Set a stake by the hold and one in deep water. Stretch wire between the two, tying the one in deep water at the bottom of the stake.

3. Prior to tying the wire to the dam stake, slip the slide wire attached to the trap onto the wire going from dam to deep water.

4. Set the trap about 12″ away from hole in the dam, which may require building a platform to hold the trap. If the trap was set right in the hole, it may get buried without ever touching the beaver.

Beaver Run Set

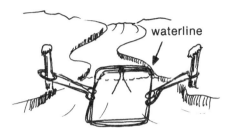

1. Stake conibear on each side as shown.
2. If water is present, set trap so the top is right at waterline.
3. Also, find where the beaver are coming *out* of the water to set. If the beaver are coming into the water and most likely will have branches to set off the trap.

Beaver Lodge Set

Find the entrance to the lodge that has fresh twigs leading to the hole.

Scent Set

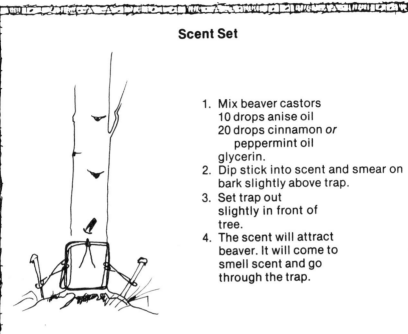

1. Mix beaver castors
   10 drops anise oil
   20 drops cinnamon *or*
       peppermint oil
   glycerin.
2. Dip stick into scent and smear on
   bark slightly above trap.
3. Set trap out
   slightly in front of
   tree.
4. The scent will attract
   beaver. It will come to
   smell scent and go
   through the trap.

Bank Hole Set

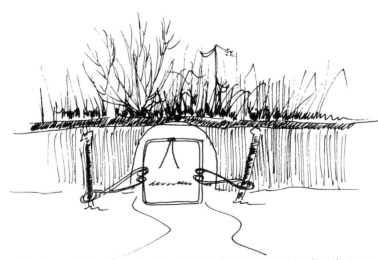

Look for large holes in bank side and for fresh chewed twigs that may
have been dragged into the hole. Then set trap as shown.

Buckskin
and
Fur Hide Tanning

3

Since the beginning of time, hide tanning has been essential to survival. Somewhere along the line, it was discovered that if the brain of the animal was made into a paste and applied to the wet hide, the hide would stretch and soften when worked over a sharp stick. Indians and a few white men use this method today.

Vegetable-tanned leather, made with tannin, a substance derived from the bark of oak trees or other vegetable materials, was and is used for footwear, belts, scabbards, cases, and even armor.

Today, commercial tanneries use a chrome tanning solution to produce garment leather because it is quicker than other methods. When this solution is used, hides will change from their natural color to a blue-green shade, so hides tanned by this method are always dyed various colors. When a hide is tanned with brains or ammonium alum, it comes out a natural white. Then, if desired, it can be oiled and smoked to obtain various shades of yellow brown and can be waterproofed either by the oils in the smoke or by other oils available commercially.

The hide tanning explanation here will deal with deer or similar sized game and fur bearing animals. I would recommend using alum because of safety, availability, and good results for clothing articles.

The alum tanning process shown here will take about 15 days from beginning to end—the dehairing taking the longest time.

When you are ready to skin the deer, hang it head down. Cut the underside of a skinning knife from neck to vent hole. Then, cut up the underside of each leg to the knee and cut around. Peel the hide from the back legs and rump. If meat or fat sticks to the hide, take a knife and keep the blade flat against the hide to shave off fat or meat. Continue until finished, but be careful not to cut into the hide, making thin spots which may tear when tanning.

The chapters on clothing will tell you how many hides you will need for each project.

Buckskin Tanning

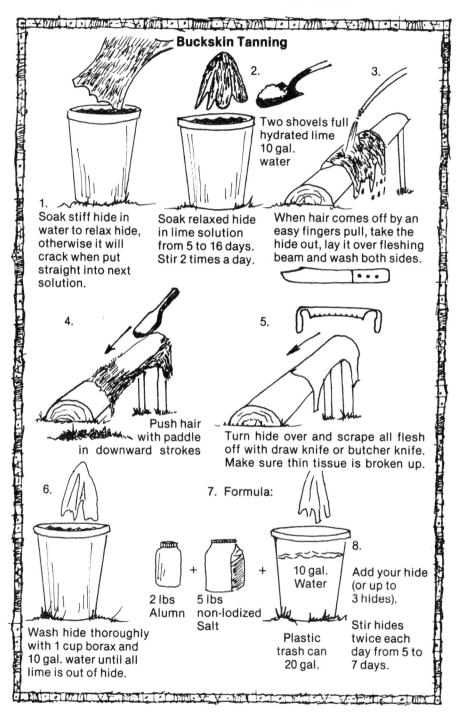

1. Soak stiff hide in water to relax hide, otherwise it will crack when put straight into next solution.

2. Soak relaxed hide in lime solution from 5 to 16 days. Stir 2 times a day.

Two shovels full hydrated lime 10 gal. water

3. When hair comes off by an easy fingers pull, take the hide out, lay it over fleshing beam and wash both sides.

4. Push hair with paddle in downward strokes

5. Turn hide over and scrape all flesh off with draw knife or butcher knife. Make sure thin tissue is broken up.

6. Wash hide thoroughly with 1 cup borax and 10 gal. water until all lime is out of hide.

7. Formula:

2 lbs Alumn + 5 lbs non-Iodized Salt + 10 gal. Water

Plastic trash can 20 gal.

8. Add your hide (or up to 3 hides). Stir hides twice each day from 5 to 7 days.

Buckskin Tanning (continued)

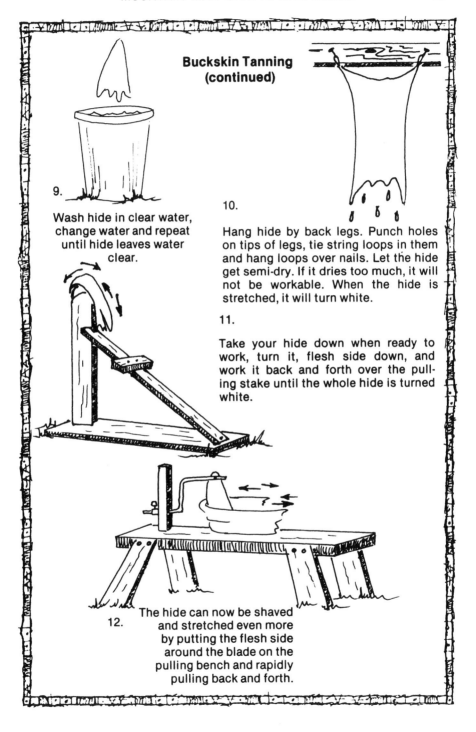

9.

Wash hide in clear water, change water and repeat until hide leaves water clear.

10.

Hang hide by back legs. Punch holes on tips of legs, tie string loops in them and hang loops over nails. Let the hide get semi-dry. If it dries too much, it will not be workable. When the hide is stretched, it will turn white.

11.

Take your hide down when ready to work, turn it, flesh side down, and work it back and forth over the pulling stake until the whole hide is turned white.

12. The hide can now be shaved and stretched even more by putting the flesh side around the blade on the pulling bench and rapidly pulling back and forth.

Buckskin Tanning (continued)

13. Re-wet the hide with a rag.

14. Sulphonated Oil

pan of warm water

1 part oil to 5 parts water

15. Rub the mixture into both sides of the wet hide.

16. Roll wet hide up, put in a plastic bag over night.

17.

Re-work hide as in steps 11 and 12. Your hide should now be soft and ready for smoking.

18.

To waterproof your hides, build a smudge fire by using rotten wood or a wood with a high grease content that will smoke without much flame and hang the hide above it high enough not to burn. The longer you smoke your hide, the more waterproof it will be.

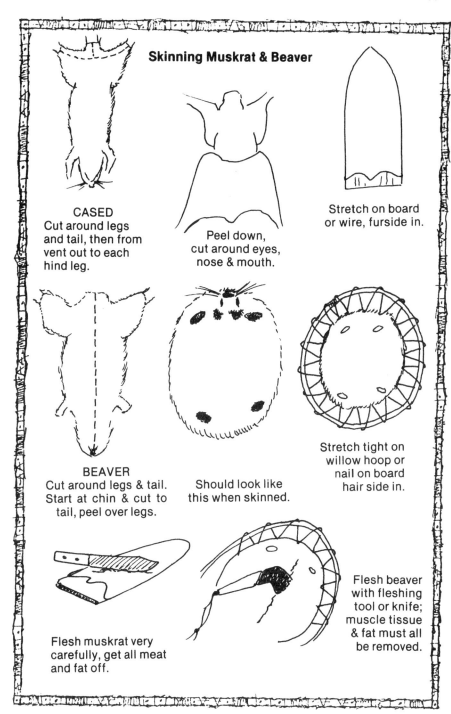

Skinning Muskrat & Beaver

CASED
Cut around legs and tail, then from vent out to each hind leg.

Peel down, cut around eyes, nose & mouth.

Stretch on board or wire, furside in.

BEAVER
Cut around legs & tail. Start at chin & cut to tail, peel over legs.

Should look like this when skinned.

Stretch tight on willow hoop or nail on board hair side in.

Flesh muskrat very carefully, get all meat and fat off.

Flesh beaver with fleshing tool or knife; muscle tissue & fat must all be removed.

Fur Tanning

Fur Tanning Formula:

Alumn 1 lb. + Salt 1 cup + Water 1 gal + Sal Soda ½ cup + Water ½ gal = Tanning Solution

Wash all dirt and grease out with ½ cup borax, 5 gal. water.

Rinse hide. Make sure hide is relaxed.

Soak hide in tanning solution 5 to 7 days. Stir 2 times a day.

Wash solution out of hide.

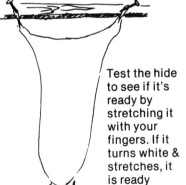

Test the hide to see if it's ready by stretching it with your fingers. If it turns white & stretches, it is ready to work.

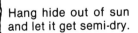

Hang hide out of sun and let it get semi-dry.

Work the hide, flesh side out, over the stake to stretch it. Keep working it until it is soft and flexible.

Fur Tanning (continued)

 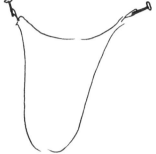

Wet the hide down again, add 1 part sulphanated oil to 5 parts warm water in a jar, shake; then soak a rag in it and rub it into the wet hide, both sides.

Roll hide up and let it sit all night.

Hang hide again and let it get semi-dry, then rework it. It will stay soft and supple now.

Wet a rag with white gas and rub into the fur to degrease it.

Rub warm hardwood sawdust into it to pick up excess gas and grease.

Let it dry, then beat with stick to get sawdust out.

Use a fine-toothed curry brush and brush fur. You now have a finished fur.

Making Rawhide

Rawhide can be made from buckskin, antelope, elk, or cow. It can be used for a number of projects such as parfleches, knife scabbards, moccasin soles, and re-inforcing wooden parts on rifles, throwing axes and bullet pouches.

If you plan to use a cowhide, cut it in half. They are very heavy and hard to handle. Other hides can be left whole.

Prepare the hide as you would for tanning. If you want your rawhide to be a whitish color, soak it in a solution of washing soda, mixing about 2 cups to the gallon of water. Soak the hide about 2 days, stirring it as often as possible. Rinse the hide out and follow the instructions on the following pages.

After tanning some hides, you may not be satisfied with the end product. This could mean that you didn't put enough elbow grease into working the hides, or maybe they weren't stirred enough in the solution for a long enough period of time.

I've had these problems and have found that the more I worked the hides, the softer they became. Sweat and good use of muscle will produce some fine quality leather and furs.

Now you are ready to put that leather and fur to good use in making some mountainman gear that will laast a lifetime.

Making Rawhide

Soak stiff hide in water to relax it. If it is put in lime solution stiff, it will crack the hide.

Hide should be soaked from 5 to 16 days until hair comes off by lightly pulling.

2 shovels full of hydrated lime to 10 gal. of water.

Lay hide on fleshing beam & rinse both sides.

With hair side up, push down with paddle to scrape hair off.

Wash in clean water until all traces of lime are out.

Turn hide over and flesh with draw knife or butcher knife. Push & scrape until meat and tissue is all off.

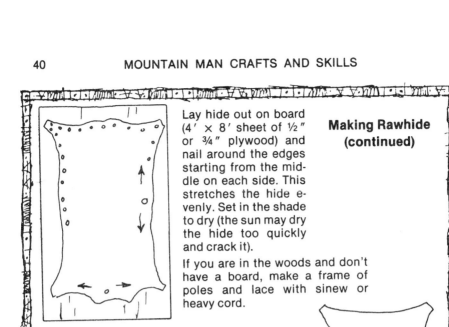

Lay hide out on board (4′ × 8′ sheet of ½″ or ¾″ plywood) and nail around the edges starting from the middle on each side. This stretches the hide evenly. Set in the shade to dry (the sun may dry the hide too quickly and crack it).

Making Rawhide (continued)

If you are in the woods and don't have a board, make a frame of poles and lace with sinew or heavy cord.

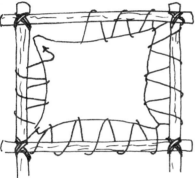

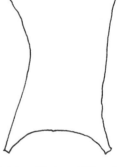

The hide will dry stiff and may be cut or trimmed to desired size.

Your scrap pieces can be used for cutting lace. Soak the piece and cut in a circular pattern starting on the outside edge.

Store hide in a shady place that is dry and free from rodents. Lay them flat on top of each other.

Rawhide can also be frozen wet without stretching it and can be used when wet. Allow for shrinkage.

MAKING MOUNTAIN MAN CLOTHING

When the fur trappers headed West, most of the clothing that they carried with them was originally made in the city and was not too practical for use in the wilderness. Within a short time, they learned that integrating Indian styles with their own could make them quite comfortable. In addition, buckskin clothing lasted longer, was tougher and more waterproof, and the producer of buckskin was always nearby.

Although buckskin shirts and pants were worn, so were muslin and wool shirts and the ever-popular red flannel long johns. Boots might have been worn in the beginning of the trade era, but the trapper soon found that moccasins could be of great value when trying to track game, allowing the trapper to feel the ground with his feet for dry branches and other objects that might make noise.

There are several advantages to making your own clothing. This type of clothing usually lasts a lifetime and teaches some necessary skills for a survival situation when it would be necessary to provide your own clothing.

Total cost in making this clothing varies so greatly that it would not be wise to make an estimate. Naturally, if you do your own tanning you will save about 85% on costs. At this writing, if you were to make a buckskin shirt, pants, moccasins, and coat, the sale value would be around $1,500 including your labor, etc. Making your own can save a lot of money.

After making your set of clothing, you'll have a rugged wardrobe that will be worth hundreds of dollars and will give you a feeling of satisfaction that you could never get by going to the store to buy them.

41

Buckskin shirts were introduced to the white man by the Indians. As the explorer started into the wilderness, he found that his fabric shirts would not endure the demands of the heavy scrub oak, thistles, and dense forests. A shirt made of thin buckskin could take the beating in the woods, shed water, and be cool in summer yet warm in winter. When he needed a new one there were generally deer in the area that could be killed and eaten, and the hide used for clothing.

Let it be understood, though, that the store-bought shirt was a prize possession of the mountain man, to be worn on special occasions, and it was always an item that was brought in from St. Louis to the Rendezvous.

The best way to start your buckskin shirt is to use a simple long-sleeved store-bought shirt pattern in your size. Tape the front pattern together and lay out the sleeve, front, and back sections on your buckskin. Tape the yoke sections to the front and back sections to get proper shirt length.

When all sections are in place, draw (with a pencil) around the edge of the pattern and cut out following the diagrams on the following pages.

If you don't have your own buckskin, cowhide will do and it can be purchased from a tannery, or leathercraft store (Tandy Leather).

If you have your own buckskin, plan on it taking about 4 hides— 1 for the front, 1 for the back, 1 for sleeves and collar, and 1 for fringe. For cowhide, measure your pattern by square feet. That is the way it is sold.

A shirt of buckskin will last a lifetime.

Buckskin Shirt

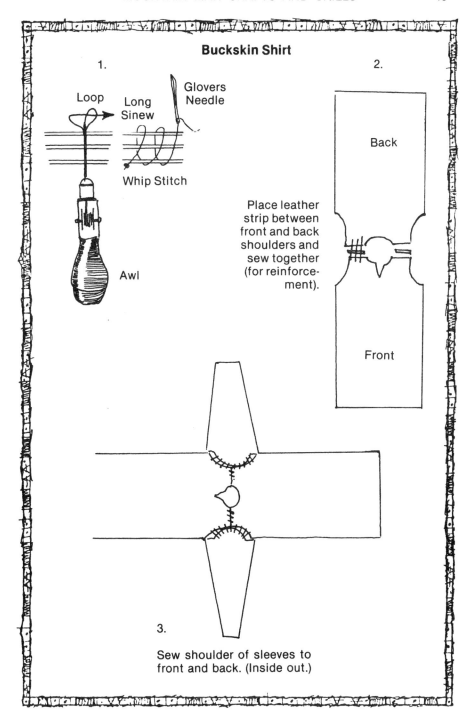

1.

Loop

Long
Sinew

Glovers
Needle

Whip Stitch

Awl

2.

Back

Front

Place leather
strip between
front and back
shoulders and
sew together
(for reinforce-
ment).

3.

Sew shoulder of sleeves to
front and back. (Inside out.)

Buckskin Shirt (continued)

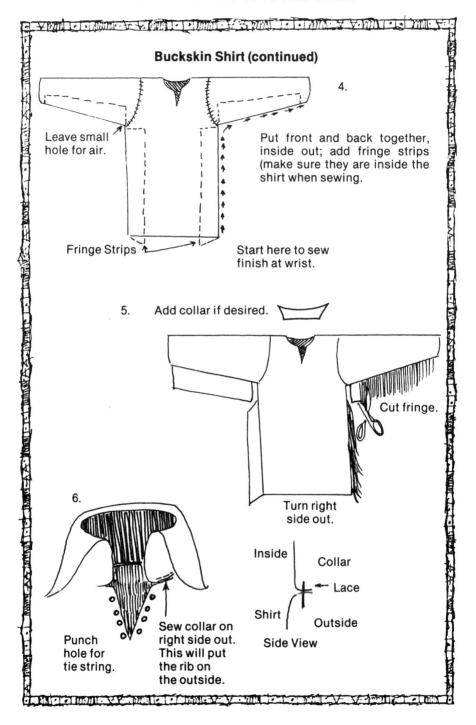

4.

Leave small hole for air.

Put front and back together, inside out; add fringe strips (make sure they are inside the shirt when sewing.

Fringe Strips

Start here to sew finish at wrist.

5.   Add collar if desired.

Cut fringe.

Turn right side out.

Inside

Collar

Lace

Shirt

Outside

Side View

6.

Punch hole for tie string.

Sew collar on right side out. This will put the rib on the outside.

Cotton or Muslin Shirts

Cotton and muslin shirts were common in the early 1800's. They were either a solid color or had a small floral print. Both shirts with collars, and collarless shirts were worn. Sleeves generally were quite full at the cuffs. The front lacing was usually leather. Many modern commercial patterns can be obtained which, with a few alterations, can be made to resemble the mountain man style. Illustrated are the pattern pieces needed with the alterations dotted in.

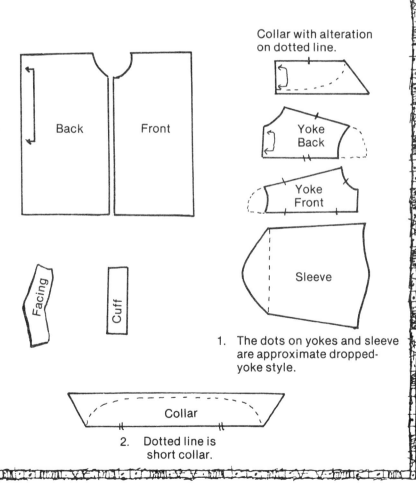

Collar with alteration on dotted line.

1. The dots on yokes and sleeve are approximate dropped-yoke style.

2. Dotted line is short collar.

Cotton or Muslin Shirts (continued)

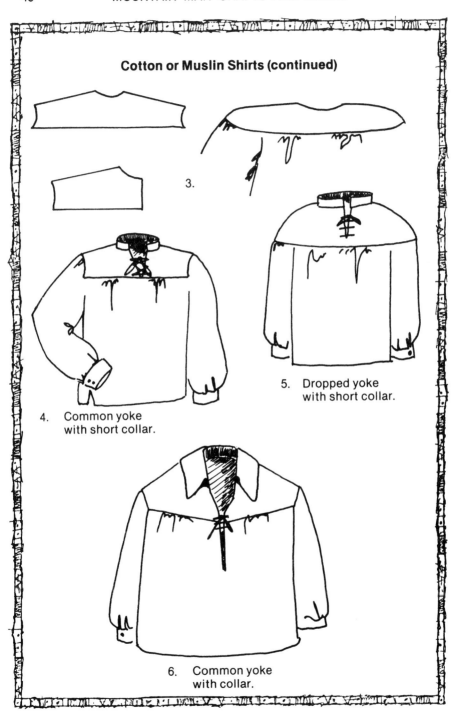

3.

4. Common yoke
   with short collar.

5. Dropped yoke
   with short collar.

6. Common yoke
   with collar.

Mountain Man Pants

The mountain man, upon arrival in the West, found that his original wool or cotton pants couldn't take the punishment of the rugged country he had come to work in. Often the Indian clothing was not exactly to his taste, so he adapted the Indians' material, leather, to his own design. Now he had a pair of pants which would last. If he were a hunter he would make long, full-length buckskins. The trapper made short ones that only came to the knee, then put leggings on from the knee down. This was so that he was able to remove the lower portion when he needed to wade into the cold water to set his traps. If he wore long-legged pants, he soon found out that they not only didn't dry quickly, but also remained cold and became stiff.

The pants you make will be up to you. Four different patterns are shown here—trapping pants or hunter's pants, with or without breechcloth.

Don't get too excited when the seat and the knees begin to bulge after awhile. It is common because leather stretches.

It will take about 4 hides of buckskin to make a pair of pants or you will have to measure the square footage of the pattern you use when purchasing cowhide.

The four designs on the following pages will show you how to make pants.

Mountain Man Pants

1. Materials needed for making the pants are: leather scissors or X-acto knife, artificial sinew, sewing awl or leather needle and either a pants pattern or an old pair of pants that can be cut off (they should still fit), plus buckskin or garment leather.

2. Take old pants apart and lay over the leather to trace with a pencil.

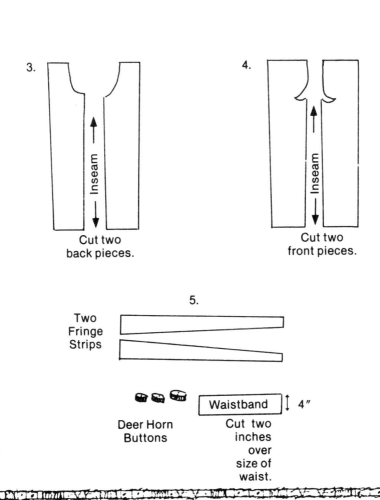

3.

Inseam

Cut two
back pieces.

4.

Inseam

Cut two
front pieces.

5.

Two
Fringe
Strips

Deer Horn
Buttons

Waistband   ↕ 4″

Cut two
inches
over
size of
waist.

Mountain Man Pants (continued)

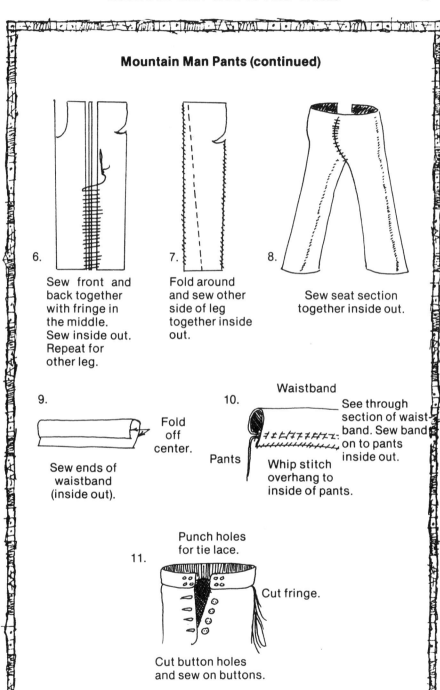

6. Sew front and back together with fringe in the middle. Sew inside out. Repeat for other leg.

7. Fold around and sew other side of leg together inside out.

8. Sew seat section together inside out.

9. Sew ends of waistband (inside out). Fold off center.

Waistband

10. Whip stitch overhang to inside of pants.

Pants

See through section of waistband. Sew band on to pants inside out.

11. Punch holes for tie lace. Cut fringe. Cut button holes and sew on buttons.

Trapping Pants

2.

Above
knee to
ankle.

1.

Make pants same as regular
pants except make them
only knee length.

Leggings

Flair at bottom.
Top must be wide
enough to
go around leg.
May be wool or
buckskin.

3.

Fold on
top & sew
leaving
hole for
drawstring.

Buckskin Leggings

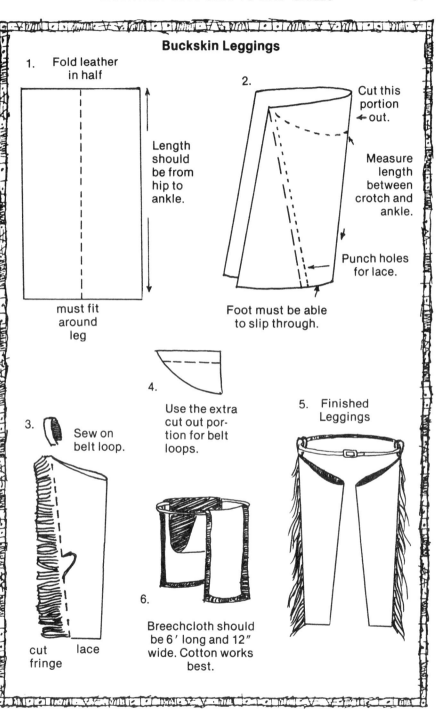

1. Fold leather in half

Length should be from hip to ankle.

must fit around leg

2. Cut this portion out.

Measure length between crotch and ankle.

Punch holes for lace.

Foot must be able to slip through.

3. Sew on belt loop.

cut fringe   lace

4. Use the extra cut out portion for belt loops.

5. Finished Leggings

6. Breechcloth should be 6' long and 12" wide. Cotton works best.

Blanket Leggings

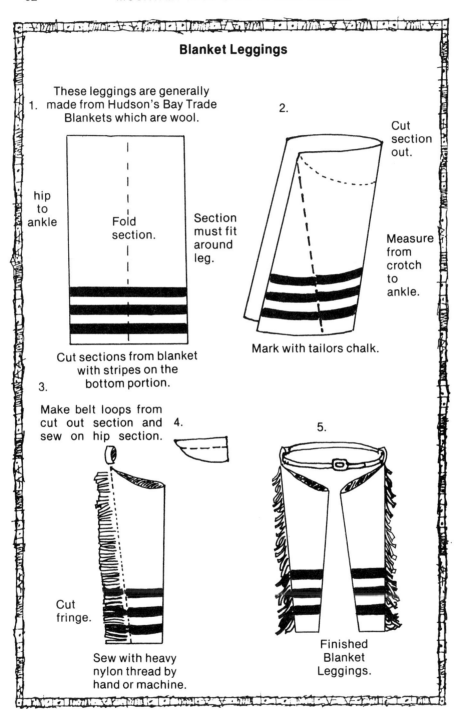

1. These leggings are generally made from Hudson's Bay Trade Blankets which are wool.

hip to ankle

Fold section.

Section must fit around leg.

Cut sections from blanket with stripes on the bottom portion.

2. Cut section out.

Measure from crotch to ankle.

Mark with tailors chalk.

3. Make belt loops from cut out section and sew on hip section.

4.

5.

Cut fringe.

Sew with heavy nylon thread by hand or machine.

Finished Blanket Leggings.

Buckskin Dress

Since few white women were included in the explorations of the West and did not have to endure the misery that the first explorers experienced, they never adopted Indian clothing, even when trekking across the plains to the West.

The Indian women lived in different circumstances than the white women, which called for a more durable type of clothing. When the white man introduced cloth to the plains Indians, the squaws would use off-red, black, and white material for some beautiful ceremonial dresses, but again buckskin was still most durable and was used for everyday wear. Many buckskin dresses were quite beautifully decorated with quillwork or, later, beadwork.

At most modern-day Rendezvous in the West, the women prefer to wear buckskin dresses and look quite beautiful in them without wigs or Indian make-up.

Although there is only one design here, you can make as many alterations as you desire, depending upon your imagination.

Measure from shoulder to knee or below the knee to get the length. Then measure the width around the chest and hips. This is a simple pattern that can be made on newspaper first, then laid on the hide and traced.

Buckskin Dress

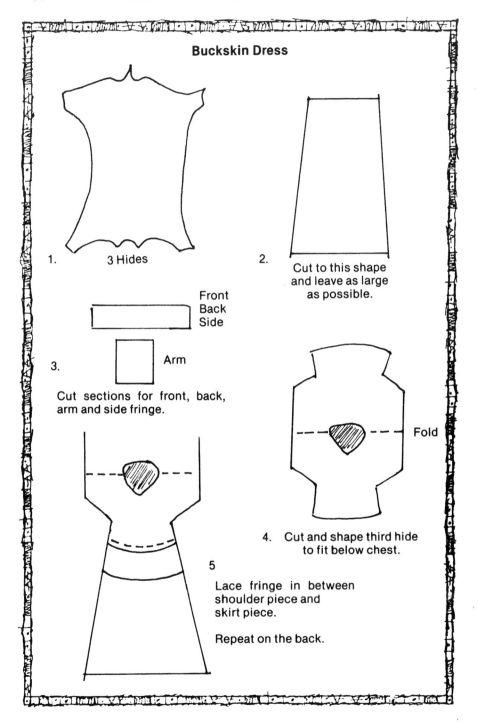

1.   3 Hides

2.   Cut to this shape
and leave as large
as possible.

Front
Back
Side

3.   Arm

Cut sections for front, back,
arm and side fringe.

Fold

4.   Cut and shape third hide
to fit below chest.

5

Lace fringe in between
shoulder piece and
skirt piece.

Repeat on the back.

Buckskin Dress (continued)

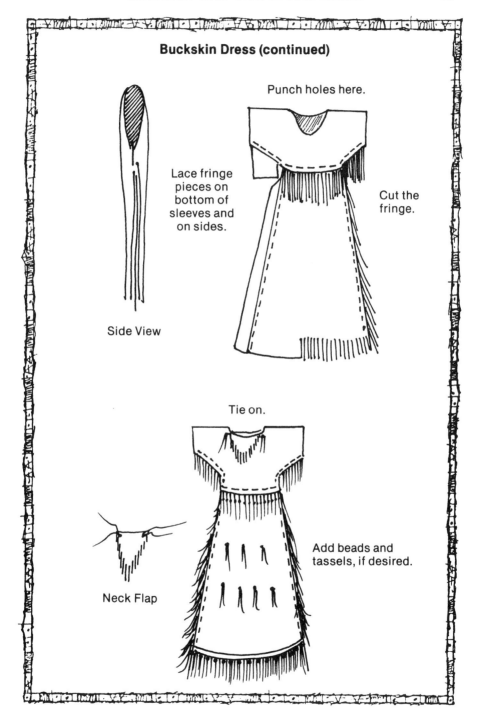

Punch holes here.

Lace fringe pieces on bottom of sleeves and on sides.

Cut the fringe.

Side View

Tie on.

Neck Flap

Add beads and tassels, if desired.

Sioux Indian Dress

When trade cloth was introduced to the Sioux, they fashioned a very pretty black, red, and white dress that was good for summer use as well as special occasions.

Today, since many mountain man activities are held in the summer, a buckskin dress would be warm, so a decorative cotton dress would be the answer to keeping cool at Rendezvous.

The material is not expensive and can be purchased at most fabric shops.

Cowrie shells can sometimes be purchased at craft stores.

The Sioux Indian Dress is made of cotton or flannel with the colors being red, black and white. It can be trimmed with cowrie shells or elks teeth if you're fortunate enough to have that many. Plastic elks teeth are made, but most people don't like to use plastic. This dress is loose, airy and quite comfortable in the summer.

Instructions

1. Make either with black body and red border or the opposite, in either case, with white ¼ " twill tape trim.

2. Measure elbow to elbow, shoulder to finished length, chest to which you need to add about five inches, and last, the head measurement to determine the neck size.

3. Layout the body fabric as shown and draw the pattern on with tailor's chalk. This dress is loose; the underarm cut should not be too shallow—midbody below the bust line is about right. It might be a good idea to have the person for whom the dress is intended to lay down on the fabric and trace the pattern around her body.

4. Open out the cut-out body fabric and trace onto paper the correct shapes for the sleeve and hem border. Then draw a large oval shape which should be at least as wide as the person's shoulders. Cut this out of paper and check it on the fabric to be sure that the shape looks good. Then cut these shapes out of the contrasting fabric.

5. Mark the head measurement with tailor's chalk onto the wrong side of the neck border. Do not cut it out yet. Lay the right side of the neck border on the wrong side of the body piece and sew around the marked neck edge. Cut out the neck hole, clip and curve, turn it to the right side, and press. Lay the right side of the arm borders on the wrong side of the body and sew the outside edge. Trim the seam, clip the corners and turn and press.

6. Sew the loose edge of both neck and arm borders. Then add the twill tape trim to both edges of the border, covering the raw edge of the border fabric.

7. Sew the dress side seams, right sides together. Turn and press. Sew the side seams of the hem border. Turn and press.

8. Attach the bottom border in the same manner as the other borders, i.e., sew hem edges, right sides together, then turn, press, sew the raw edge down and add trim.

9. Sew the decorations on by hand, using as few or as many as desired. Sew the bottom edge of the sleeve together in at least three places with the decoration, one on each side.

Sioux Indian Dress

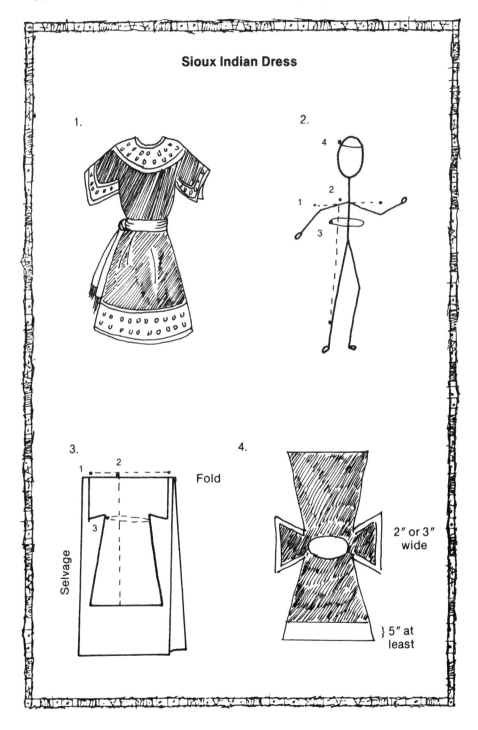

1.

2.

3.

Fold

Selvage

4.

2″ or 3″ wide

} 5″ at least

Sioux Indian Dress (continued)

5.

6.

7.

8.

9.

Moccasins

There are many styles of maccasins and many books detailing their construction. Therefore, only the styles most popular with the mountain men are illustrated here. These styles can have innersoles to cushion the step. This is excellent footgear to wear when stalking deer or other game. The plains moccasin is best suited to plains or woodland terrain and the Apache style is best suited to more rocky country because of the heavier sole.

It would be best to make the patterns on butcher paper first to make sure of proper fit. Use either a heavy buckskin or cowhide to make the mocassins, particularly when making one piece moccasins. Latigo for soles on the others will have to be purchased at a leather supply store or a tannery. It is tanned and heavily oiled and thick. Tack shops use it to make saddles.

If you are going to go out in the snow or wet weather, make sure your moccasins are well oiled. I use a mink oil-beeswax solution. Heat and melt the wax right into the oil. Using a paint brush, paint the solution on the mocassins.

Moccasins can't be beat for stalking wildlife because of the softness of the soles which conform to the surface where you are walking.

One Piece Plains Moccasin

1. Begin by drawing pattern of foot on the flesh side of soft leather.

2. Locate the point 1 about ½ " from the tip of the toe.

3. Draw a line 1 to 5 about 1½ " long.

4. Draw line 1, 2, 3 ¼ " from sole out- line at point 2. At 3 it should be 3" from the center of the heel and ¼ " below it.

5. Draw line 3 to 4, about 6".

6. Cut out drawing that is made and fold over on dotted line 4 to 5.

7. Draw around cut edge for the other side and cut out.

8. 7 and 8 are flap cuts at an angle 6" long.

9. 9 and 10 are ½ " deep and 1¼ " wide.

10. Fold so that points 6 and 3 touch and sew (inside out) from point 5 to 1, 2 & 3 then the back of the heel.

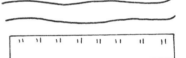

11. Cut two strips of leather 2" wide and long enough to go around the top.

12. Cut slots for drawstring and sew to top of moccasins.

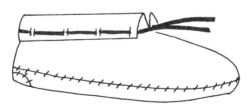

13. Insert drawstrings and the moccasins are ready to wear.

Apache Style Moccasins

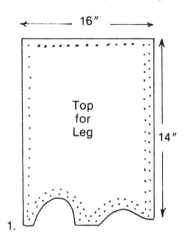

16″

Top
for
Leg

14″

1.

Cut according to pattern and use awl to punch holes.

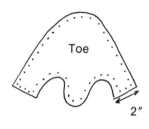

Toe

2″

2.

The toe and heel have to be measured according to the length of the sole.

DOUBLE ALL PIECES

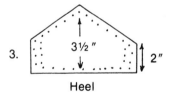

3½″

2″

3.

Heel

4.

Latigo sole size at foot plus ½″ all the way around.

5.

Leather insole size of foot.

Apache Style Moccasins (continued)

Top portion should be 16″
long and cut as shown.

6.

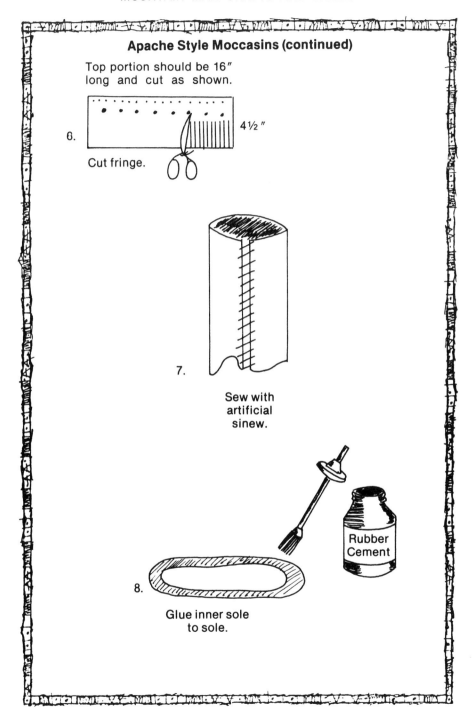

4½″

Cut fringe.

7.

Sew with
artificial
sinew.

Rubber
Cement

8.

Glue inner sole
to sole.

Apache Style Moccasins (continued)

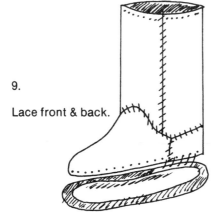

9.

Lace front & back.

Sew sole to top
starting in the
middle of the insole.

10.

Sew on fringe and
insert draw string.

Wool Booties for Moccasins

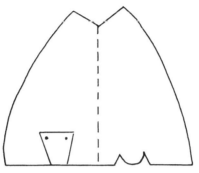

1.

Cut and follow same instructions as for the Plains Moccasins using scrap pieces from a blanket, coat or similar heavy wool.

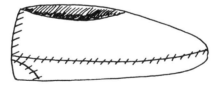

2.

Do not add the extra top piece. These will keep your feet good and warm in the winter when wearing Apache-style moccasins.

Two Piece Plains Moccasin

Double all sections. Make
a paper pattern of all parts.

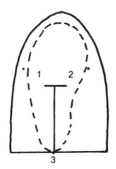

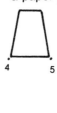

1. Draw outline of foot on paper and add ¼ " all around foot outline. Cut sole from this outer line.

2. Make upper portion ½ " longer than sole. The width depends on the size of your foot. Measure with tape over the top of the boot to find the width.

3. Cut T-shape as in diagram, try on foot and if it fits, cut leather the same size.

4. Sew sole onto top, inside out.

5. Sew tongue on and add inner sole.

6. Add draw string.

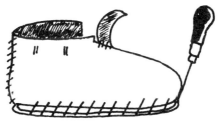

Buckskin Coat, Lewis and Clark Style

Warm, durable and weatherproof are the terms that best describe this coat. When the exploration for the northwest passage took place, no one really knew what conditions lay ahead. To prepare for all contingencies, only the best clothing, that considered to be the most durable and the most suitable, was taken along. A coat was needed that could protect man from the freezing torrential rains of the plains, and from alpine snows. One that was tough enough to take the scrapes of sharp rocks and the snags of hard springy limbs was also needed. This coat, with its beaver fur collar, shoulder cape, and heavy buckskin material, met all of these needs and could last a lifetime.

After having made such a coat with my home tanned buckskin and beaver pelts, I have had numerous compliments on it and it is one of the most popular projects in the book. Although it takes a lot of hides, it will be well worth it. My coat has been valued at about $1,000.

You can make the coat shorter or longer, as you desire. Use different fur on the collar or leave the trim off the sleeves and bottom. At this point, you can begin altering the designs to fit your personal taste and needs.

Buckskin Coat

1. Make all patterns out of paper first. Portions may be taken from commercial patterns, such as the arms.

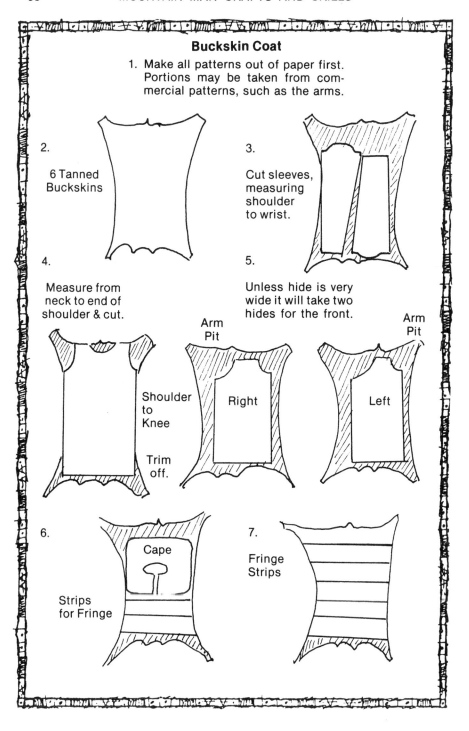

2. 6 Tanned Buckskins

3. Cut sleeves, measuring shoulder to wrist.

4. Measure from neck to end of shoulder & cut.

5. Unless hide is very wide it will take two hides for the front.

Shoulder to Knee

Trim off.

Arm Pit

Right

Arm Pit

Left

6. Strips for Fringe

Cape

7. Fringe Strips

Buckskin Coat (continued)

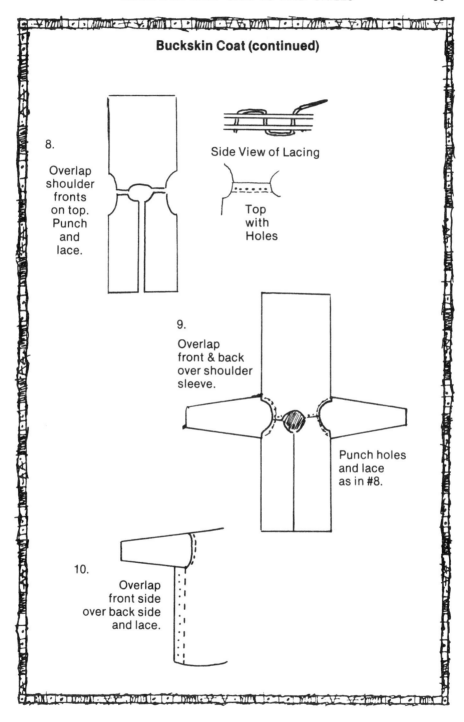

8.

Overlap shoulder fronts on top. Punch and lace.

Side View of Lacing

Top with Holes

9.

Overlap front & back over shoulder sleeve.

Punch holes and lace as in #8.

10.

Overlap front side over back side and lace.

Buckskin Coat (continued)

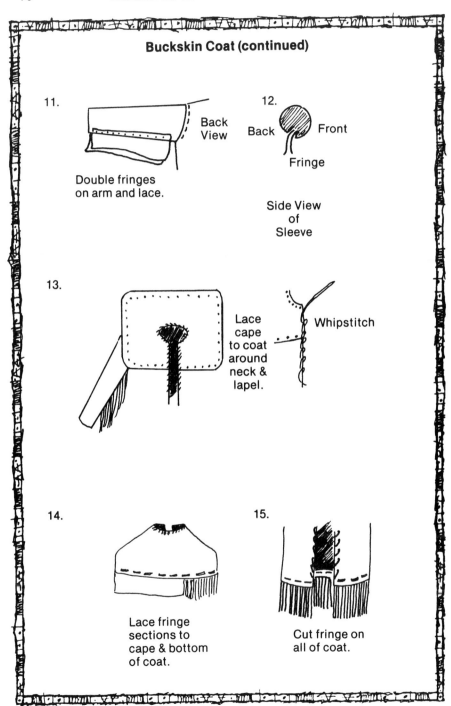

11.

Back View

Double fringes on arm and lace.

12.

Back   Front

Fringe

Side View of Sleeve

13.

Lace cape to coat around neck & lapel.

Whipstitch

14.

Lace fringe sections to cape & bottom of coat.

15.

Cut fringe on all of coat.

Buckskin Coat (continued)

16. 66″

Tanned
Beaver Pelt

17. Do not use
scissors. Use
an X-acto knife
and cut from
the flesh side
to avoid
damaging hair.

Cut sides and
back as shown.

18.

Sew Pieces of
beaver collar
together on
back side.

19.

Sew collar on to coat
with sinew using existing
lace holes.

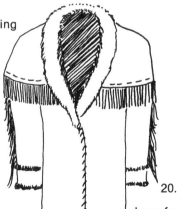

20.

Lace front edges of coat
and trim cuffs and bottom
with beaver fur.

Finished
Coat

Capote
(Blanket Coat)

The Hudson Bay Company was established in the territories of England to establish a fur trade with the Indians. Among one of the prized trade items was the Hudson Bay 4-point trade blanket. When the Indian obtained one of these blankets, it was then cut and sewn into a hooded coat that could keep the chill off at low winter temperatures.

This coat, used by both Indians and Mountain men, is a good all-weather warm coat which can stand heavy usage. Typically, it was made from a Hudson Bay Blanket, but any good quality woolen blanket will do. The instructions for making the coat are as follows.

Instructions

1. Enlarge the pattern onto a large piece of paper. Several sheets of newspaper taped together will do. Make sure that the measurements for the back length, A to E, and for the sleeve length, A to C and C to F are accurate. Take the sleeve measurement as shown in the drawing with the arm at the side.

2. Lay out the pattern pieces on the blanket which has been folded in half lengthwise. Adjust the pieces on the strips to obtain the best proportions. After cutting out the body and the hood and tassels, the sleeve pieces may be folded in half to facilitate cutting.

3. With right sides together, using a 5/8" seam, sew the shoulder seam CD.

4. With right sides together sew the underarm seam DG.

5. Place the sleeve in the armhole with the wrong sides together, the sleeve extending into the body and the fringe sticking out of the armhole. Align the seam lines, CD, sew and cut the fringe.

6. With right sides together, sew the hood seam H I placing the small ends of the tassels in the seam at point I with the tassels on the inside.

7. Fold the hood fringe back to the outside along line BJ and stitch ½" from the fold and hold it in place. Cut the fringe.

8. To sew the hood to the capote, place the right side of the hood to the wrong side of the capote making sure to match points B. Point A on the body should match point H on the hood at the center back. Stitch, cut the fringe, which will fold back to cover the stitching, and whip stitch the inner seam allowance to the capote.

9. On the outside, cover the armhole and shoulder seams with the grosgrain ribbon.

10. Bind all the raw edges of the front and cuff with ribbon and the front edge of the hood as well. The hem may be finished with ribbon, or a fringe may be cut, whichever is desired.

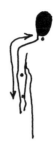

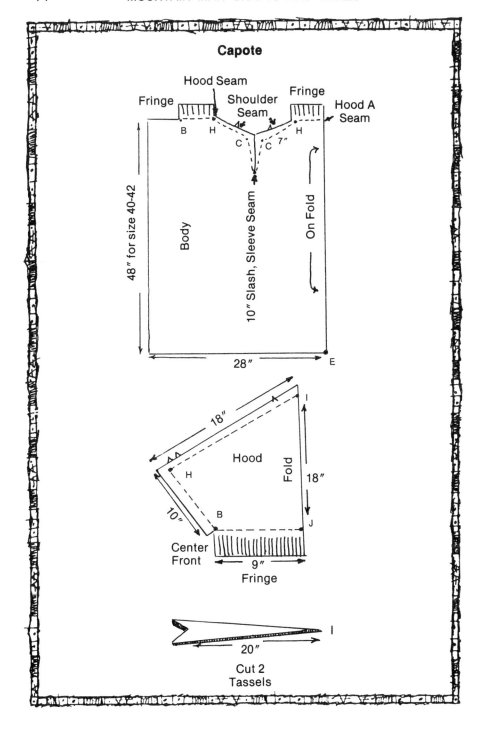

Capote

Hood Seam

Fringe   Shoulder Seam   Fringe   Hood A Seam

B   H   C   C 7″   H

Body

48″ for size 40-42

10″ Slash, Sleeve Seam

On Fold

28″   E

Hood

18″

Fold

18″

H

B   J

10″

Center Front

9″

Fringe

I

20″

Cut 2
Tassels

I

Capote (continued)

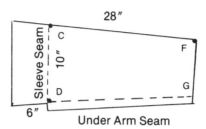

28″

Sleeve Seam

C

10″

D

6″

F

G

Under Arm Seam

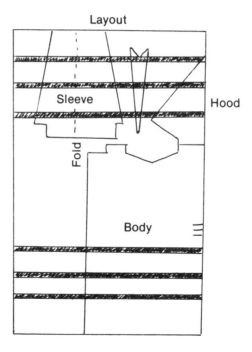

Layout

Sleeve

Hood

Fold

Body

Capote (continued)

Belts and Sashes

A mountain man did not think of a belt as we do today. He did not use his belt to keep up his pants. He used a drawstring or suspenders for that purpose. Instead, he used his belt as a means of carrying his belt pouch, strike-a-light pouch, knife or ax, or whatever he needed to carry. Many times the coats that they wore had no buttons but were kept closed by a belt or sash. Also, sashes were more decorative and sometimes used for special occasions in the Indian manner.

In order for you to compete in most mountain man activities today, you will need a belt to hold a belt pouch, knife scabbard and throwing ax.

Good belt leather can be obtained at leather craft stores in different lengths and widths. Buckles too, may be obtained at the same place or you can make your own out of plate steel if you have the equipment necessary to do the work.

Sashes are good for tying the capote shut or your buckskin coat, and can be made from scrap blanket or cotton.

Belts and Sashes

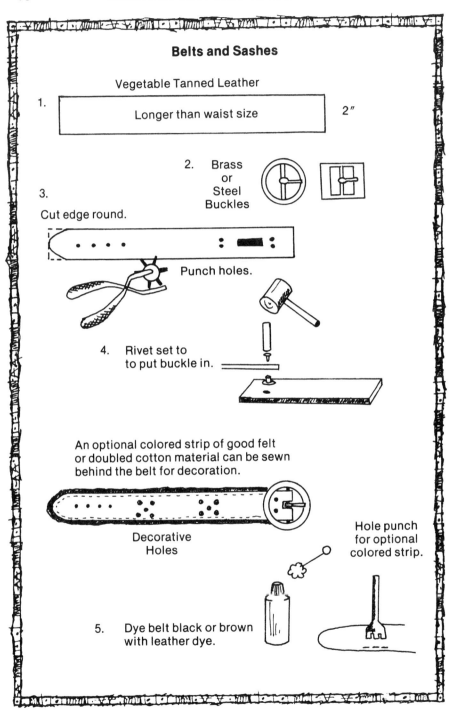

Vegetable Tanned Leather

1.

Longer than waist size

2"

2. Brass
or
Steel
Buckles

3.

Cut edge round.

Punch holes.

4. Rivet set to
to put buckle in.

An optional colored strip of good felt
or doubled cotton material can be sewn
behind the belt for decoration.

Decorative
Holes

Hole punch
for optional
colored strip.

5. Dye belt black or brown
with leather dye.

Belts and Sashes (continued)

Sashes can be made of soft buckskin, cotton or wool. They can be made any length desired.

1.

5″

2. Fold and sew
    adding fringe on each end.

3. If bead work is added, Make
    the bead work on a loom first
    and then attach to sash.

Beaver Mittens

Mittens are much better than gloves, due to body heat and also are easier to get on and off when trapping. Although other types of furs can be used, beaver is best for repelling water and also has a nice soft cushy down. A trigger finger is added on for convenience in hunting.

1. Trace an outline of
   your hand on a sheet
   of paper and cut it out.

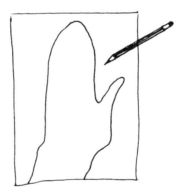

Beaver Mittens (continued)

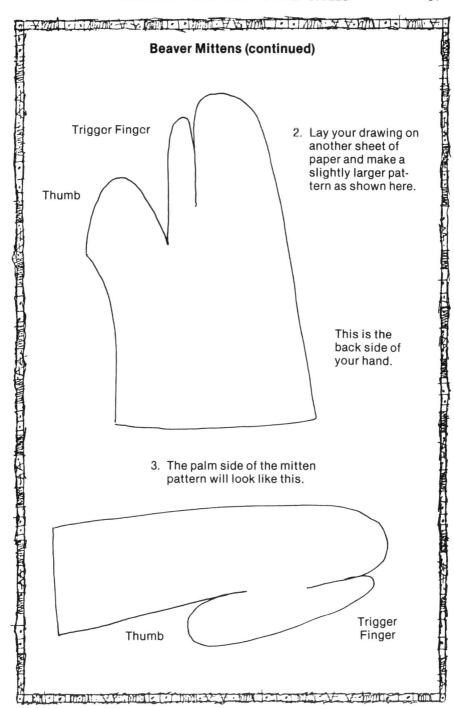

Triggcr Fingcr

Thumb

2. Lay your drawing on another sheet of paper and make a slightly larger pattern as shown here.

This is the back side of your hand.

3. The palm side of the mitten pattern will look like this.

Thumb

Trigger Finger

Beaver Mittens (continued)

4. Take a medium size tanned beaver hide and lay out your pattern on the flesh side and trace it on. Cut it out and reverse for the other hand.

5. Take a glovers needle and a strong nylon thread and sew mittens as close to the edge as you can. Do this inside out.

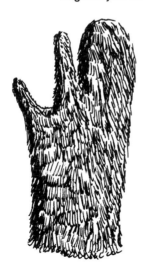

6. Turn right side out and you have your finished mittens.

Snowshoes

If you have completed at least a shirt, pants, and moccasins, you are well on your way to being able to complete many of these other projects at a much faster pace and each project will become easier as you become more experienced.

You will eventually find that you will want to design your own style of clothing to suit your tastes. The craftsman who can eventually make a set of clothing out of all home tanned leather will be the envy of his peers and will be proud to know that the clothing he wears, although it took a lot of sweat to tan and sew, cannot even be compared to the factory tanned, store-bought leathers many wear today.

Snowshoes

Today, snowshoes can be purchased at most sports stores and they come in traditional wood and rawhide, metal and plastic. The mountainman found that snowshoes were a must if he were to get his winter trapping done.

The snowshoes shown here are green willow and rawhide. Other woods can be used.

1. Rawhide should be cut in long thin strips and kept wet while lacing.
2. Cut willows 1″ thick with the sides at least 3½ feet long.
3. Tie, let dry, and varnish. This will prevent rawhide from softening up.

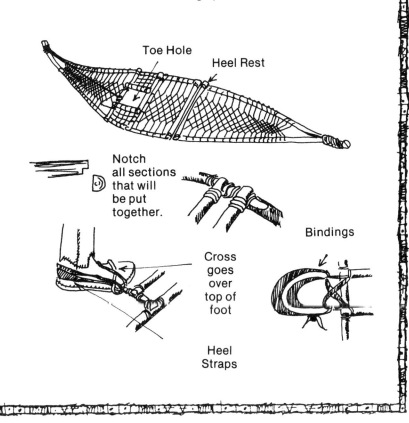

Toe Hole

Heel Rest

Notch all sections that will be put together.

Bindings

Cross goes over top of foot

Heel Straps

Rifles,
Knives and
Throwing Ax

To the mountain man, his rifle, knife, and hatchet or ax was essential to his survival in the wilderness.

His rifle was used for the taking of game for food and for protection against hostile Indians. The knife was as important due to the fact that he not only had to skin and cut up the meat he shot for food, but also was a necessity for skinning and fleshing the all important beaver he trapped.

The ax used by the trapper served to cut limbs for trapping stakes, firewood, and briskets or big game. He used this as well as the knife for throwing contests at Rendezvous time.

All three of these items can be obtained at most Black Powder shops. Rifles are available at most large sporting goods stores, knives through cutlery firms or at Rendezvous and the ax, which is more difficult to find, only at Black Powder shops or Rendezvous.

A black powder magazine called, *The Buckskin Report,* Box 885, Big Timber, Montana 59011, has information in their ad section on places to obtain these articles.

The cost for these vary greatly depending on the quality you want. Rifle kits range from about $100 to $300. Knife kits are from $3 to $20, and axes from $13 to $100.

Rifles

From at least 1811 to the 1820's the "squirrel rifle" was the most commonly used rifle among the trappers and traders. The Kentucky has a long heavy muzzle and was a small caliber bore which was not sufficient for the big game animals of the wilderness. No wonder, a chance meeting with a "grizz" in the early days almost always met with certain doom if the hunter tried to shoot it.

Eventually the U. S. Rifle, M1803 with a 34" barrel and a .52 caliber found its way into the hands of a few trappers. Finding these to work better than the Kentucky, the halfstock became popular and some kept theirs as flintlocks while others converted to percussion.

A few wise gunsmiths picked up on the desires of the mountain men and became well known intheir day for manufacturing a superb plains rifle. Two of these were the Hawken brothers in St. Louis. They produced a standard half stock, 34" octagonal barrel, .53 caliber, percussion lock, with "snail" enclosed nipple, set trigger, low sights, steel butt plates and thimbles for the ramrod. It weighed about 10½ to 12 pounds. Hoffman, J. F. Diettrich and Hellinghaus also produced reputable rifles at that time.

It is not the intent in this section on rifles to instruct how to build one but to familiarize the new mountain man with the styles, names, parts of the rifle and black powder safety. Also brand names of kits you can purchase that have adequate instructions for building your rifle.

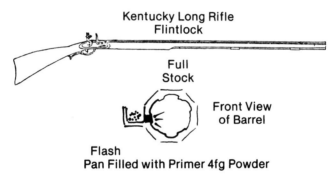

Kentucky Long Rifle
Flintlock

Full
Stock

Front View
of Barrel

Flash
Pan Filled with Primer 4fg Powder

Rifle Building

Rather than instruct on how to build a rifle in this book, which by the way would take a book in itself, some of the companies are listed here that have kits as well as parts for .45, .50, and .54 caliber Kentucky and Plaines rifles:

> Connecticut Valley Arms (CVA)
> Thompson/Center Arms
> Hopkins and Allen
> Lyman
> Browning Arms
> Navy Arms

Rifle Building (continued)

Lock   Jaw   Frizzen

Spring

Flash
Pan

Sights

Ramrod   Thimbles   Cap

Hawken Plains Rifle
Cap Lock

Half Stock

Rifle Building (continued)

Lock   Hammer   Nipple   Snail

Set Trigger

Loading the Rifle

1. Using 2 or 3 F powder, pour powder into set measurement (according to your specific rifle). Powder Measure.

2. Pour powder into barrel. Make sure hammer is set on nipple.

Rifle Building (continued)

Short
Start

Spru
is Up

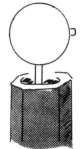

Wet Patch

3. Lay precut patch
center over barrel.
Lay ball on top, spru
side up, and tap
into barrel with
short start.

4. With long end of short
start, ram ball in.

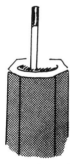

Cap

6. Pull hammer back to
safety, put #10 or #11
cap on nipple.

5. With ramrod, seat
ball and patch
against the powder.

Trigger Adjustment Screw

Set Trigger

Trigger

7. When you have weapon against the shoulder,
pull set trigger, then hammer, then trigger to shoot.

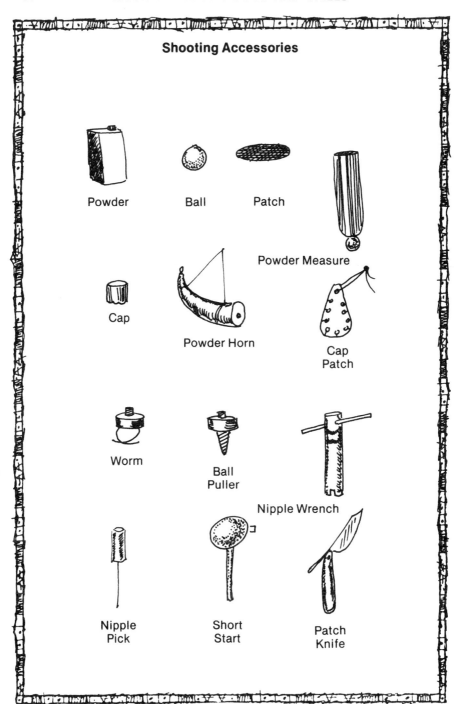

Short Starts

An essential part of your shooting gear is a short start. After the powder is poured into the barrel, the patch and ball must be forced down to seat on the powder. It is quite a struggle to start a ball with just the ramrod and many ramrods are broken in this manner. The ball must be tapped in and then pushed part way down so that the long ramrod will be easier to use to get the ball properly seated. Some short starts, as the one illustrated here have a very short piece to tap the ball in and another to get it started down the barrel.

Wooden Short Start

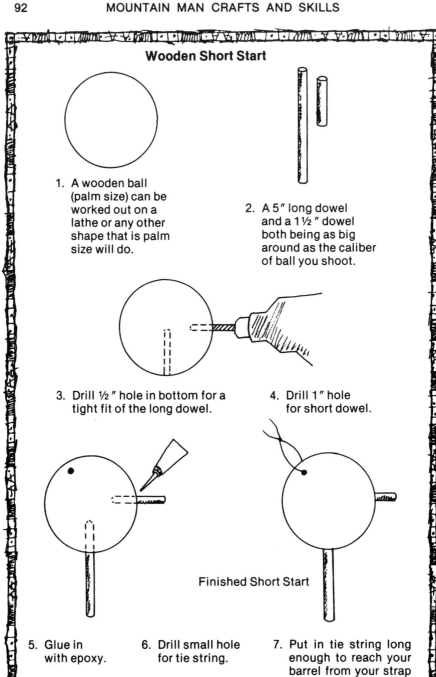

1. A wooden ball (palm size) can be worked out on a lathe or any other shape that is palm size will do.

2. A 5″ long dowel and a 1½″ dowel both being as big around as the caliber of ball you shoot.

3. Drill ½″ hole in bottom for a tight fit of the long dowel.

4. Drill 1″ hole for short dowel.

Finished Short Start

5. Glue in with epoxy.

6. Drill small hole for tie string.

7. Put in tie string long enough to reach your barrel from your strap on your possibles bag.

Horn-Handled Short Start

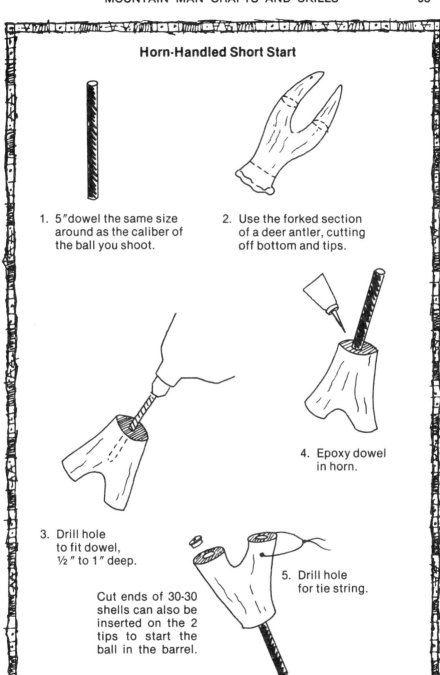

1. 5" dowel the same size around as the caliber of the ball you shoot.

2. Use the forked section of a deer antler, cutting off bottom and tips.

4. Epoxy dowel in horn.

3. Drill hole to fit dowel, ½" to 1" deep.

Cut ends of 30-30 shells can also be inserted on the 2 tips to start the ball in the barrel.

5. Drill hole for tie string.

Cleaning Your Rifle

It is important that a black powder weapon be cleaned after each day of shooting as the powder is very corrosive. Take the barrel off the stock, set it in a bucket of hot soapy water, put a rag patch on the end of a cleaning jag. Push the patch down the barrel and as you pull it up, it will draw the water up the barrel. Continue to do this, changing patches until the patches come out clean. Take the nipple off and clean it in soapy water. Rinse the barrel with hot water, swab it with alcohol, and then oil it well. Take the lock off and clean it, oil it and wipe it dry. Assemble all parts and put the rifle in the scabbard, never put it in an airtight case.

Black Powder Safety

It is wise to keep in mind regular rifle safety rules as well as the special cautions concerning black powder use.

1. Never point your rifle at another person even if you know the rifle is not loaded.

2. Treat your rifle as if it were always loaded.

3. When crossing fences, always have your hunting partner hold the rifle, or, if out alone lay your rifle on the ground, not against the fence.

4. When walking with someone, walk single file with the rifle crossing the arms.

5. Never overcharge your barrel, follow the amount of grains recommended for the rifle you are using.

6. Blow any sparks out of the barrel prior to reloading.

7. Always use the right size patch and ball.

8. Do not carry a cap on the nipple when walking.

9. Always hold the side of the ramrod rather than hitting the end with your palm when pushing it down the barrel. Rods are known to break and if for some reason there happens to be a live spark in the barrel it could blow the ramrod through the palm of your hand.

10. The ball *must* be seated against the powder. If it is not, the barrel will blow because of the air pocket.

11. Never take the breech plug out. If you must have it out, have a gunsmith do it.

12. *Always* remember to take the ramrod out of the barrel before shooting. It is not uncommon to see someone, in the heat of

competition, shoot a ramrod at the target, and I'm speaking from experience.

13. When shooting on a range with others, always keep the rifle pointed down range.

14. Never fire on a range until the range officer hollers "range clear."

15. Don't use the rifle as a hammer.

16. Always be sure of your target.

17. Black powder rifles are not toys! They can kill.

18. Know your powder storage regulations in your area. Black powder is a high explosive and should be treated as such.

19. Always keep your powder dry.

20. Never walk on to a range unless a range officer has stopped the shooting.

Mountain Man Shoot

When it comes to Rendezvous time, it's time to get out the Hawken or Kentucky or whatever kind of black powder weapon you have (cannons too) and sharpen up your aim. One of the main attractions of rendezvous is the keen competition on the range.

If there is a good "booshway" in charge of the rendezvous, the shooting contests will be challenging and creative. The shoots illustrated here will serve any beginning group as well as the old timers and will provide much enjoyment. Most of the target silhouettes are made of thick steel so that they can be reused. The distances vary on how far the targets are from the shooter, but a good 25 to 30 paces away is about average.

Shoots

A Square 2-Man Shoot

1st man shoot to mark square. 2nd man tries to hit first man's mark.

2-Man Team Shoot

Buffalo Shoot: First team to get all their buffalo down wins.

Turkey Shoot

Split Ball Shoot

Double-end ax in middle, clay pigeon on each side. Ball must break both clay pigeons when split.

Individual shooter must holler "gobble", one of 3 heads pop up, shooter has 3 seconds to get turkey down.

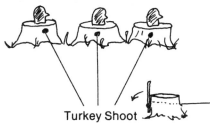

Patch Knife Shoot

Shooter closest to center wins.

Ham Shoot

Shooter must cut string with one shot. Ham or weight hung on tripod.

Cracker Shoot
Pistol

First 3 crackers hit wins.

Shoots (continued)

Tombstone Shoot

Shooter must load and shoot on back, rest barrel on tips of toes or side of foot. 1st with all three down wins.

Triangle Shoot

Try to get 3 shots (one in each corner) without hitting black. The three holes farthest apart wins.

Team Board Shoot

3-man team, 1st team to cut board in half across white line wins.

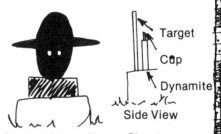

Target

Cap

Dynamite

Side View

100 Yard Sharpshooter Shoot

This should only be done if someone is knowledgeable about dynamite. Cap is set in between eyes which will set off dynamite.

Paper

1 gal. Can

Lead in Bottom

Candle Light Shoot

Shooter must shoot flame out without hitting candle. This is done in the dark.

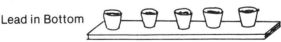

Flour Cup Shoot

Shooter can continue shooting until he misses.

Shoots (continued)

Tube Shoot

Shooter must get bullet through cardboard tube & punch the paper at the end of it.

Hawken Shoot

Buffalo is about 3′ × 4′. Shooter must hit in circle 150 yards away. He may rest his rifle.

Ax Throw

Seven natural steps away. Hit the center.

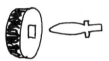

Knife Throw

Hit center.

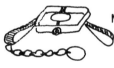

Mountainman Run

1. Set #3 or #4 trap in creek.

2. Start fire with flint and steel.

3. Run to station #3, shoot 5 gal. can at 50 yards.

4. Run to station #4, shoot can at 75 yds.

5. Run to station #5, shoot 5 gal. oan at 100 yards.

6. Run to #6, shoot can at 25 yards.

7. Run, cross wide portion of creek, throw ax and stick it.

Each man is timed. He gets two shots per target. If targets are missed, he is penalized one minute per target. This course should be in rough terrain.

Knives

Naturally there were many different styles of knives used during the mountain man era as there has been throughout time. It would take an entire book to tell the history and styles that existed at that time. The styles shown here are Green River knives which became popular in the 1830's. They come in kit form and can be ordered directly from the Green River Works in Southridge, Mass. The firm is the oldest cutlery works in the US and is very reputable.

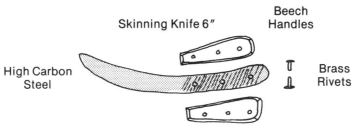

Skinning Knife 6″

Beech Handles

High Carbon Steel

Brass Rivets

1. Put handles on tang, put in rivets with hammer, making sure the rivets are straight when setting.
2. File excess steel around handle.

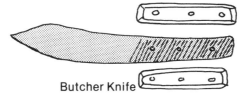

Butcher Knife

Same as skinning knife.

All kits come with rivets, blades and handles.

Knives (continued)

Hardwood
Handles

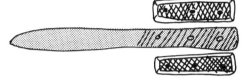

Dadley

Good for slicing, slashing or plunging
for deep cuts in an animal.

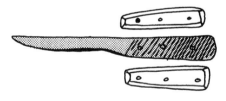

Boning Knife

For roasts and fowl.
Good fillet knife.

The Throwing Ax

The Mountain Man needed a small ax to cut fuel for his fire, to pound stakes for his traps, and as an alternate source of protection in addition to his rifle. Today the mountain man occasionally uses his ax for cutting, but mainly it is used for throwing. At Rendezvous time along with all the other competition there is always an ax throwing contest.

The place to pick up a thowing ax would be a black powder specialty shop or on traders row at a rendezvous. To find a good throwing ax, pick it up, hold the helve away from you so you look down at the eye and bit. Check to see that the bit is straight. Many times they are not and it will not be balanced for throwing. The broader the bit, the better the chance of it sticking when you throw it.

To throw an ax, set up a cut log on its side, step off seven natural paces, turn, hold on to the end of the helve, with the bit facing the target of course, and throw overhand. Keep your eye on the target and be sure to follow through as you let go.

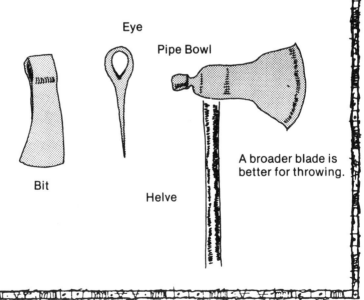

Eye

Pipe Bowl

A broader blade is better for throwing.

Bit

Helve

Rifles, Knives, and Hatchets

When considering the purchase of a rifle, make sure you know what you plan to use it for and what will suit your needs. Are you going to hunt big game, small game, or target shoot, or both? Some prefer a lighter rifle for competition and a larger one for hunting. The best way to start is with one that will serve both purposes.

I've ended up with several knives, due to different uses. I use my Dadley for big game cutting and cleaning, my skinner for skinning, and my butcher knife for meat cutting and fleshing hides. If you want a general purpose knife, the Dadley is most likely your best bet.

The ax is used mainly for throwing contests, but can also be used for cutting small limbs of firewood, and cutting the brisket off big game as I do. They are fun to throw and it's a challenge for anybody to hit the target dead center.

All three are important to your participation in mountain man Rendezvous events.

Mountain Man Hats

Tradition calls for the mountain man to wear a "coon skin cap," but in reality the mountain man and pioneer wore all types of head-gear depending on what was available and the time of the year. The French trapper wore the stocking cap that folded on the top with a tassle on the end. The other explorers and traders wore felt hats in the summer because it was cooler and kept the sun out of their eyes, and fur hats in the winter for warmth. Some of these fur hats had the animal's tail attached for decoration, be it coon, fox, coyote, skunk, etc. Some of these hats had ear flaps and leather visors. Occasionally mountain men even got their names by the hat they wore.

My first hat was made of badger and was very awkward to wear because it was poorly constructed, but I learned from it and made my next hat out of the first beaver that I trapped and it is a perfect fit.

Your hat should suit your taste as well as considering what you're going to use it for. If you're going to be wearing one just at Rendezvous time, which is usually in the summer, a good felt hat would shade the eyes as well as being cooler than a fur one. If you're a trapper, you may want a warmer hat for winter, my favorite being the one shown on the first pages of hats.

If you're not a trapper, you may need to find a furrier in your area to obtain a fur for your hat. If you live in an area where a Good-will Industries type store is located, check there. Sometimes, the fur is removed from used coats and is sold very inexpensively.

Hats can be a conversation piece as well as practical. One thing for sure, make sure it is a comfortable fit or you will be miserable and unhappy.

Hats

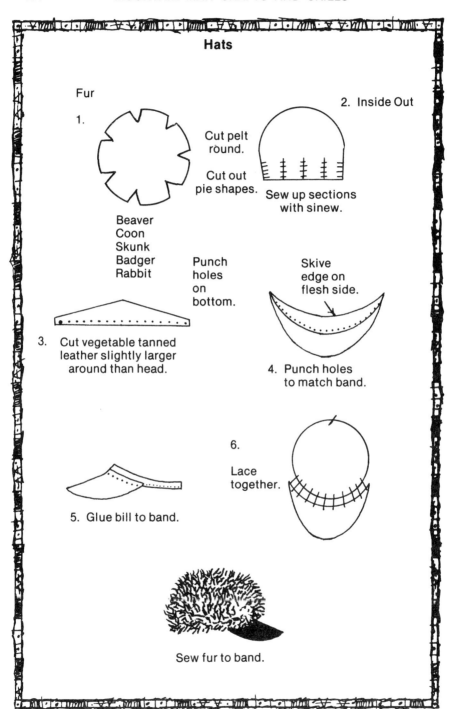

Fur

1.

Cut pelt round.

Cut out pie shapes.

2. Inside Out

Sew up sections with sinew.

Beaver
Coon
Skunk
Badger
Rabbit

Punch holes on bottom.

Skive edge on flesh side.

3. Cut vegetable tanned leather slightly larger around than head.

4. Punch holes to match band.

6.

Lace together.

5. Glue bill to band.

Sew fur to band.

Simple Fur Cap
with Ear Flaps

Side

Front

Ear Flaps

Sew with a
simple whipstitch.

Right side out with
flaps down. The flaps
can be tucked up
inside when not needed.

"Coon Skin" Cap

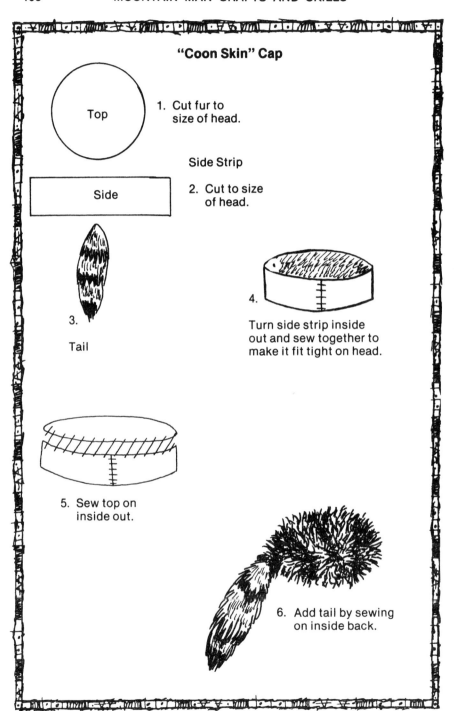

Top

1. Cut fur to size of head.

Side Strip

Side

2. Cut to size of head.

3.

Tail

4.

Turn side strip inside out and sew together to make it fit tight on head.

5. Sew top on inside out.

6. Add tail by sewing on inside back.

Beaver Felt Hat

1. After stretching and drying pelt, shave off all fur.

2. Using a piano wire stretched above a board about 4", put fur under wire and twang wire; it will make the guard hairs stand up. When this happens, take them out leaving only the down.

3. Boil the down in water.

Wooden Form Size of Head

4. Use a wooden frame the thickness you desire (1/8" is sufficient). Size around is up to you. (Don't use plywood.)

Wooden Mallet

5. Put (hot) wet down on mold. Pound felt tight and flatten on form. Let dry and sand.

Sew leather sweat band on inside.

6. Finished Beaver Hat

Other Types
of Trappers Hats

French Trappers
Stocking Cap

Regular Felt
Hat

Tuck in
shoulder, sew.
Add quilted
hat liner for
a more com-
fortable fit.

Fox or Coyote
Hat

7

Homemade Knife

Several knives can be made out of a saw blade and they work fine for skinning and butchering. They are simple to make and can be made into any shape desired. Wood, horn, or antler can be used for the handle as well as micarta for scrimshaw.

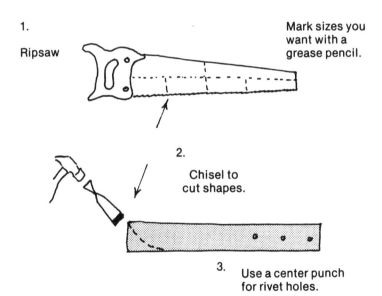

1.

Ripsaw

Mark sizes you want with a grease pencil.

2.

Chisel to cut shapes.

3. Use a center punch for rivet holes.

This particular way of knife making is for the person who wants to go beyond a kit knife and yet doesn't have access to machinery for making the fancy stainless steel blades.

The finished product will be pleasing to you and give you many years of good use.

Homemade Knife (continued)

4. Drill holes to rivet
size and a countersunk
spot on each one for
rivet heads.

5. Cut in half
with band saw.

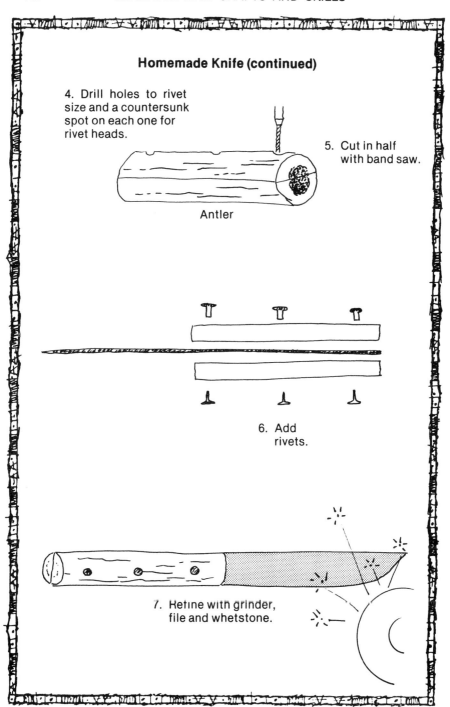

Antler

6. Add
rivets.

7. Refine with grinder,
file and whetstone.

8

Powder Flask
and
Horns

When gunpowder was first introduced, it had to be carried in some type of container. Since plastic and other artificial containers didn't exist then, horn, bone, wood, and leather were made into containers for powder.

One of the most popular methods in the early 1800's to carry powder for the rifle was a cow horn, scraped thin enough to see the level of powder through the horn.

Flasks of leather and metal were used as well, particularly for pistols.

If you have a flinklock, it requires a finer powder for the flash pan, so a primer horn (small horn) will be needed.

Horns and the leather are inexpensive, easy to do, and nice looking when properly done.

Remember to never pour your powder directly into the barrel from the horn. Always use a measure to get the exact amount needed into the barrel.

Leather Powder Flask

This type of powder flask is particularly good for the pistol shooter. It can be hung either from the neck or from the belt. It can also take quite a beating because it is made from heavy leather.

Leather Powder Flask

1.

2.

← 4″ → 5″ ← 4″ →

1. Brass or copper tube.

2. Wooden plug.

3. Vegetable tanned tooling leather.

4. Cut to shape.

5. Punch holes for lacing.

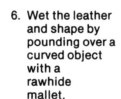

6. Wet the leather and shape by pounding over a curved object with a rawhide mallet.

7. Insert tube and glue with epoxy.

8. Lace.

9. Insert Plug

Finished Powder Flask

Powder Horns

Horns can be obtained from most slaughter houses and most will be very rough and require a lot of fileing. Most black powder shops will carry finished horns that are imported from Mexico which will save considerable work (finished horns mean, they are sanded and polished, but not assembled).

1. Cut end off with hacksaw.

2. Measure for plug.

3. File off rough surface with rough file and then fine one.

4. Sandpaper with medium then fine sandpaper.

Soften horn by boiling in can.

5. Set wood plug in softened horn and glue.

Powder Horns (continued)

6. Cut tip off.

7. Drill hole (make sure you don't drill through side of horn).

8. Make plug for powder pouring end.

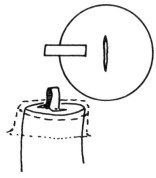

9. Take two pieces of leather as in diagram, place loop in slots, glue to plug, wrap brass wire around leather

OR

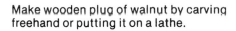
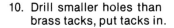
Make wooden plug of walnut by carving freehand or putting it on a lathe.

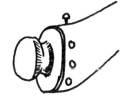

10. Drill smaller holes than brass tacks, put tacks in.

Powder Horns (continued)

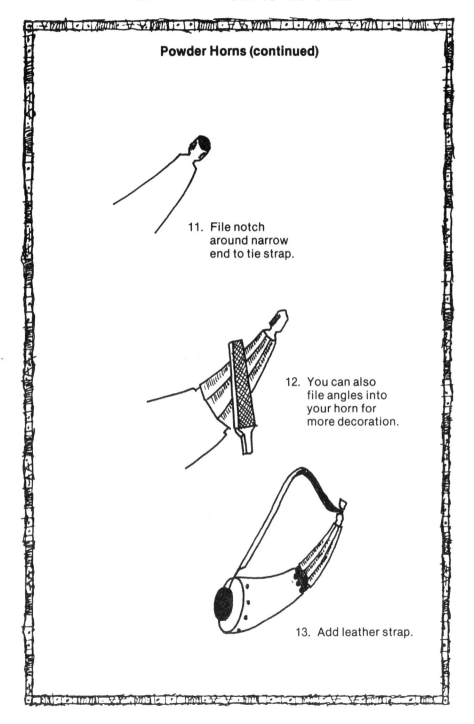

11. File notch around narrow end to tie strap.

12. You can also file angles into your horn for more decoration.

13. Add leather strap.

Flintlock Primer Horn

Prior to the cap and ball, the flintlock was the main black powder weapon. In order to ignite the powder in the barrel, a spark must enter the touch hole, and the quicker the better. For this purpose a finer grained powder (ffff) is generally used in the pan than in the barrel. Most flintlockers have two horns, one for each powder. Some flintlock shooters use the same powder in their flash pan as they use in their barrels, thus eliminating two horns.

The brass nipple is not absolutely necessary but helps put the exact amount needed on the flash pan. These can be purchased at black powder gun shops or ordered through various catalogues.

Flintlock
Primer Horn

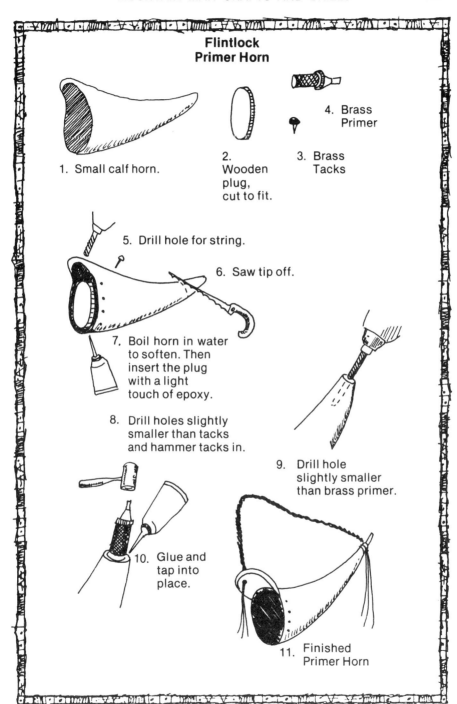

1. Small calf horn.

2. Wooden plug, cut to fit.

3. Brass Tacks

4. Brass Primer

5. Drill hole for string.

6. Saw tip off.

7. Boil horn in water to soften. Then insert the plug with a light touch of epoxy.

8. Drill holes slightly smaller than tacks and hammer tacks in.

9. Drill hole slightly smaller than brass primer.

10. Glue and tap into place.

11. Finished Primer Horn

9

Scrimshaw

Scrimshaw and horn carving has been in existence since man has. Powderhorns were carved by the Norsemen in the 1600's and by Revolutionary War soldiers. Sailors were proficient at it in the 1600-1800's. It was found that if a good supply of whalebone and ivory were kept on board ships, it kept idle hands busy and also made the sailor some extra money when he landed on the eastern seaboard.

Scrimshaw, for the mountain man, meant a record in map form of where he trapped and whatever decoration he desired to put on his horn.

Today, many attempt to scrimshaw their powder horns, but few succeed because they have no idea how to go about it. It isn't hard if you have a pre-drawn design that you can trace on and engrave.

The supplies are inexpensive and can be purchased at most art stores. It is not necessary to use an etching needle. Dissecting needles and other sharp objects will work as well.

The patterns in this section are for your convenience to copy or trace. There are many books in the public libraries that have pictures to use for ideas.

You need not confine your scrimshaw to powder horns. Ivory and micara have better surfaces to work on. These can be used as knife handles or jewelry pieces. Let your imagination go with this and create your own piece of scrimshaw. Have fun!

Scrimshaw

1. Tools and Materials

   Etching needle, tube of block-printing ink, soft lead pencil, Krylon clear acrylic spray, and design.

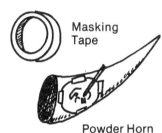

Masking Tape

Rags

Powder Horn

2.

After the horn has been sanded and finished with steel wool, spray with Krylon.

3. Trace pattern onto tracing paper, turn pattern over and use a soft-lead pencil to cover the back side.

Scrimshaw (continued)

4.

Tape pattern to horn
and trace over pattern
with hard-lead pencil.

5. Remove pattern and
   begin to scratch
   where the pattern is.

6. When scratching, make as
   long a line as possible rather
   than short, sketchy marks for
   outlines. If short lines are
   needed for hair on animals,
   do it systematically.

7. Put ink on rag
   and rub into
   scratches.

Scrimshaw (continued)

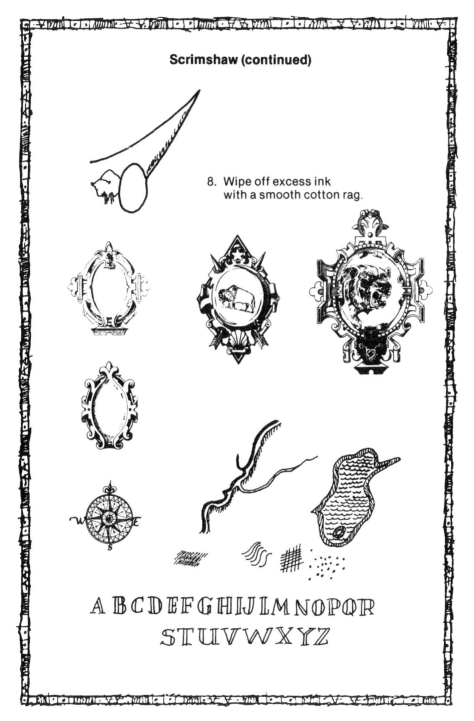

8. Wipe off excess ink with a smooth cotton rag.

A B C D E F G H I J L M N O P Q R
S T U V W X Y Z

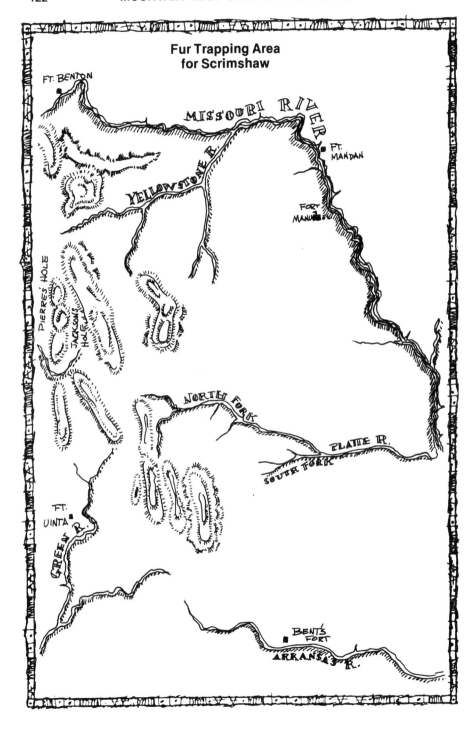

Fur Trapping Area
for Scrimshaw

Forts for Scrimshaw

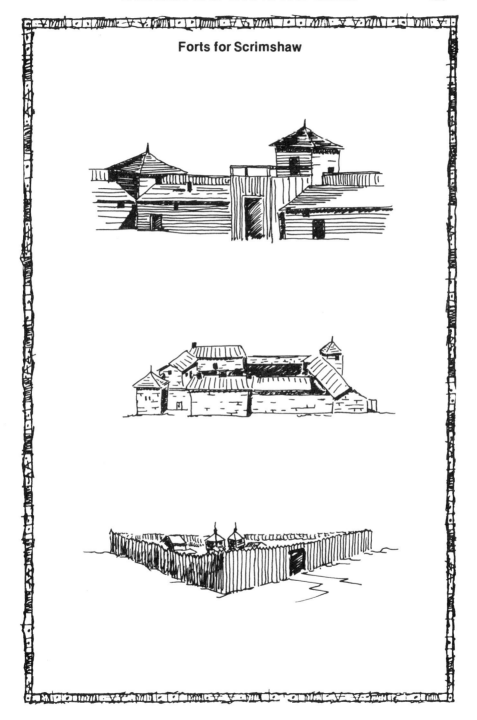

Animals for Scrimshaw

Mule Deer

Elk

Antelope

Moose

Beaver

Buffalo

Fox

Muskrat

Bighorn Sheep

Bald Eagle

10

Deer and Cow Horn Uses

Deer and cow horns can be used for numerous items that are decorative and useful. Only a few of the essential items are shown here. Some of the other things that can be made are combs, spoons, and jewelry. Use your imagination in creating what you can from these natural items.

Deer horn is easy to obtain after the deer hunt if you live in a deer hunting area. Either go to the slaughter house or a neighbor if you see that they have a deer and ask if they plan to use the deer horn. If not, offer to take it off their hands, cutting the horn under the rosette next to the skull. Leg bones can be used also for awls.

Cow horns are numerous at slaughter houses and most places will give them to you. These horns are usually thick and need a lot of refining. You can use them thick for jewelry pieces, cups, etc.

Usually a saw, file, sandpaper, and drill are all the tools you need.

Bone & Horn Use

Bone Awl

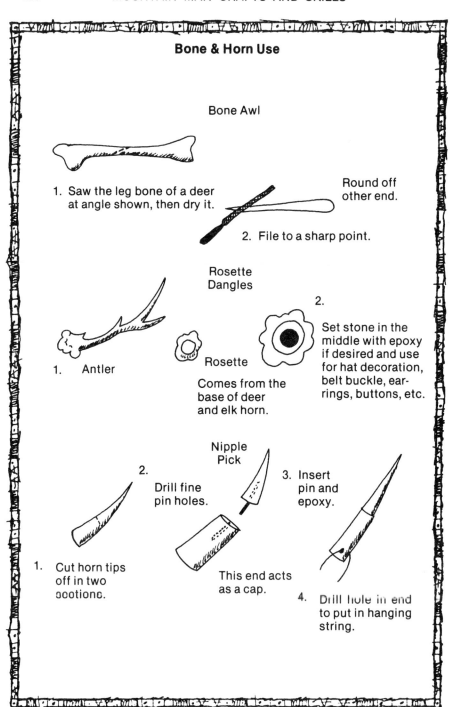

1. Saw the leg bone of a deer at angle shown, then dry it.

Round off other end.

2. File to a sharp point.

Rosette Dangles

1. Antler

Rosette

Comes from the base of deer and elk horn.

2.

Set stone in the middle with epoxy if desired and use for hat decoration, belt buckle, earrings, buttons, etc.

Nipple Pick

2. Drill fine pin holes.

3. Insert pin and epoxy.

1. Cut horn tips off in two sections.

This end acts as a cap.

4. Drill hole in end to put in hanging string.

Deer Horn Jewelry

1.

Cut section
off horn.

2.

Drill out
middle

3. Drill hole in top
and bottom,
thread with
leather, bead,
and feather for
braid or earring
dangles.

Horn Buttons

1.

Cut with a
band saw or
hacksaw.

2. Drill small
holes for
thread.

Deer Horn Jewelry (continued)

3. Buttons can also be sanded
   or filed around the edges.

Notice that the end of the
horn is worked prior to
being cut. It is much easier
to handle this way.

4. Then buffed and polished
   with an electric
   buffer.

5. Then cut, and
   torched around the edges.

Flame

6. Drill buttonhole.

Horn Powder Measure

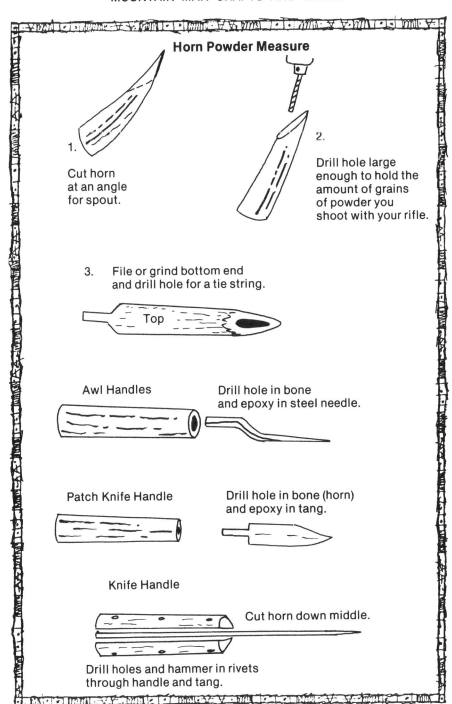

1. Cut horn at an angle for spout.

2. Drill hole large enough to hold the amount of grains of powder you shoot with your rifle.

3. File or grind bottom end and drill hole for a tie string.

Top

Awl Handles

Drill hole in bone and epoxy in steel needle.

Patch Knife Handle

Drill hole in bone (horn) and epoxy in tang.

Knife Handle

Cut horn down middle.

Drill holes and hammer in rivets through handle and tang.

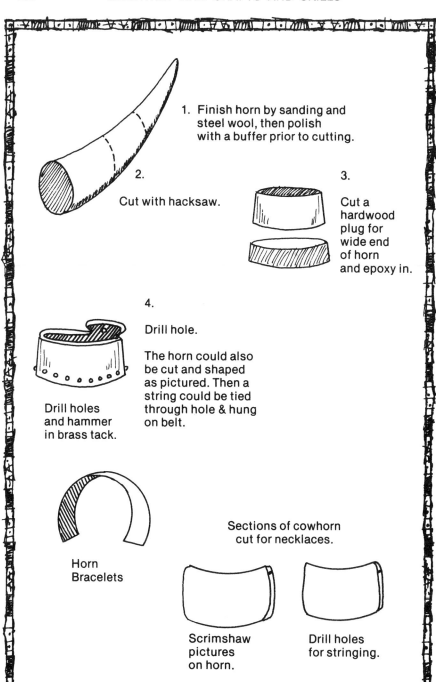

1. Finish horn by sanding and steel wool, then polish with a buffer prior to cutting.

2. Cut with hacksaw.

3. Cut a hardwood plug for wide end of horn and epoxy in.

4. Drill hole.

The horn could also be cut and shaped as pictured. Then a string could be tied through hole & hung on belt.

Drill holes and hammer in brass tack.

Horn Bracelets

Sections of cowhorn cut for necklaces.

Scrimshaw pictures on horn.

Drill holes for stringing.

11

Pouches

The mountain man carried various pouches with him, such as a possibles bag, bullet pouch, and sometimes a strike-a-lite pouch.

These pouches are for your convenience and can be made from scrap pieces of leather.

The possibles bag is to carry all your valuables, such as caps, extra balls, patches, nipple wrench and pick, flints, and tidbits to eat, etc.

The strike-a-lite pouch is made to carry your flint and steel plus your tinder bark. If you put your tinder box in the top section, it won't slap on your leg. Put cedar or sage bark in a plastic sandwich bag and place it in the lower pouch. If your pouch gets wet, your bark will still be dry.

Rather than carrying all your bullets loose in your possibles bag, make a pouch for them that you can have readily available to get bullets out quickly, such as a neck pouch.

These pouches are necessary if you are to compete in any shoots or do hunting with black powder.

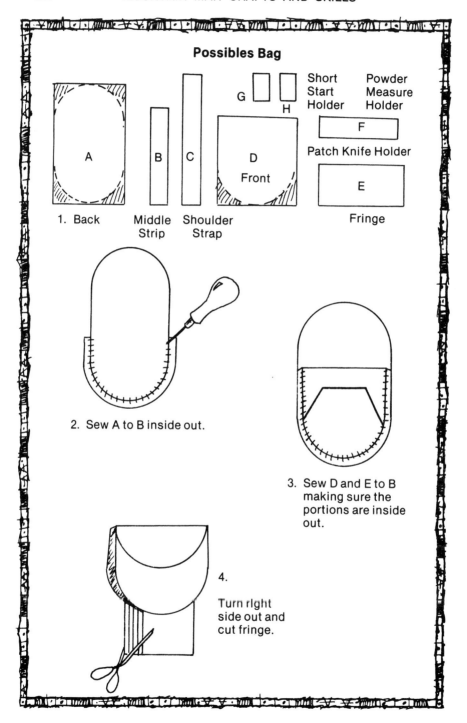

Possibles Bag

G — Short Start Holder
H — Powder Measure Holder

A — 1. Back
B — Middle Strip
C — Shoulder Strap
D — Front
F — Patch Knife Holder
E — Fringe

2. Sew A to B inside out.

3. Sew D and E to B making sure the portions are inside out.

4. Turn right side out and cut fringe.

Possibles Bag (continued)

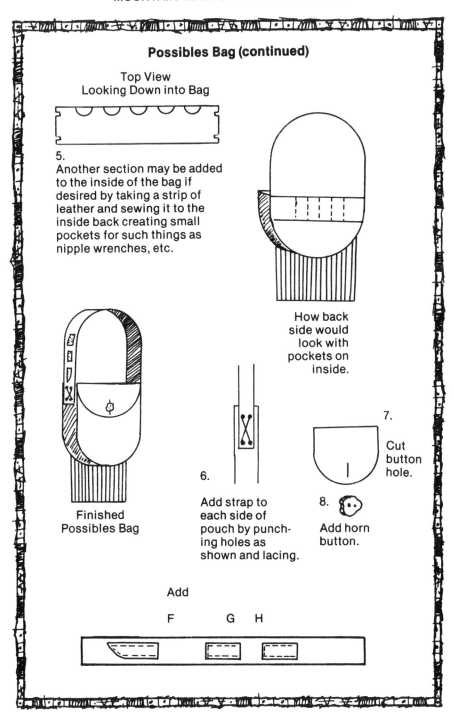

Top View
Looking Down into Bag

5.
Another section may be added
to the inside of the bag if
desired by taking a strip of
leather and sewing it to the
inside back creating small
pockets for such things as
nipple wrenches, etc.

How back
side would
look with
pockets on
inside.

Finished
Possibles Bag

6.

Add strap to
each side of
pouch by punch-
ing holes as
shown and lacing.

7.

Cut
button
hole.

8.

Add horn
button.

Add

F   G   H

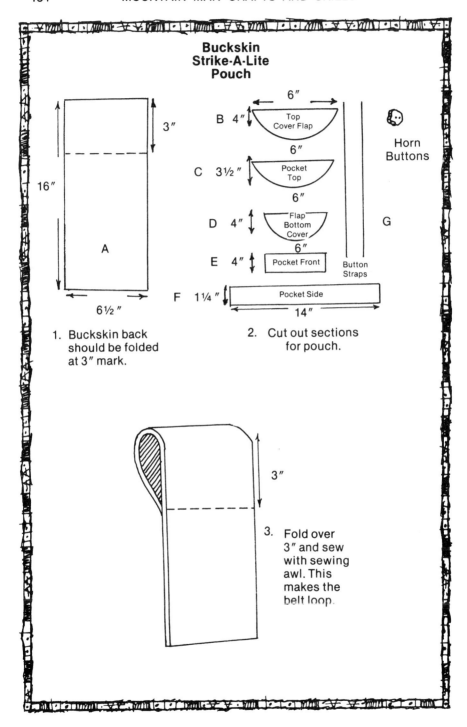

Buckskin Strike-A-Lite Pouch

16″

3″

A

6½″

B   4″   6″   Top Cover Flap

C   3½″   6″   Pocket Top

D   4″   6″   Flap Bottom Cover

E   4″   6″   Pocket Front

F   1¼″   Pocket Side   14″

Button Straps   G

Horn Buttons

1. Buckskin back should be folded at 3″ mark.

2. Cut out sections for pouch.

3″

3. Fold over 3″ and sew with sewing awl. This makes the belt loop.

Strike-A-Lite Pouch (continued)

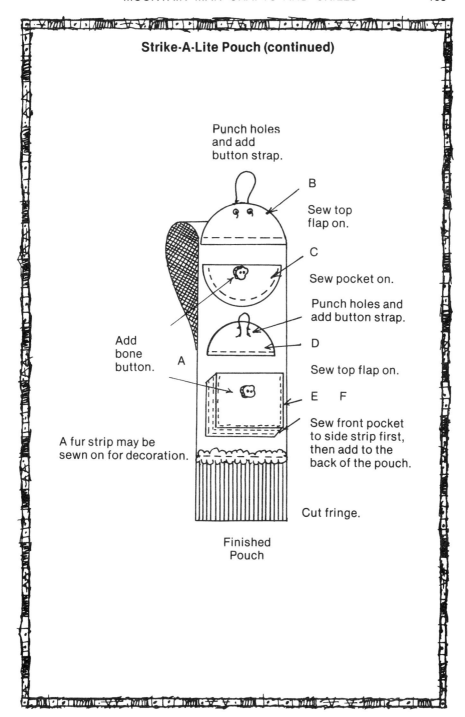

Punch holes
and add
button strap.

B

Sew top
flap on.

C

Sew pocket on.

Punch holes and
add button strap.

D

Add
bone
button.

A

Sew top flap on.

E   F

Sew front pocket
to side strip first,
then add to the
back of the pouch.

A fur strip may be
sewn on for decoration.

Cut fringe.

Finished
Pouch

Buckskin Neck Pouch

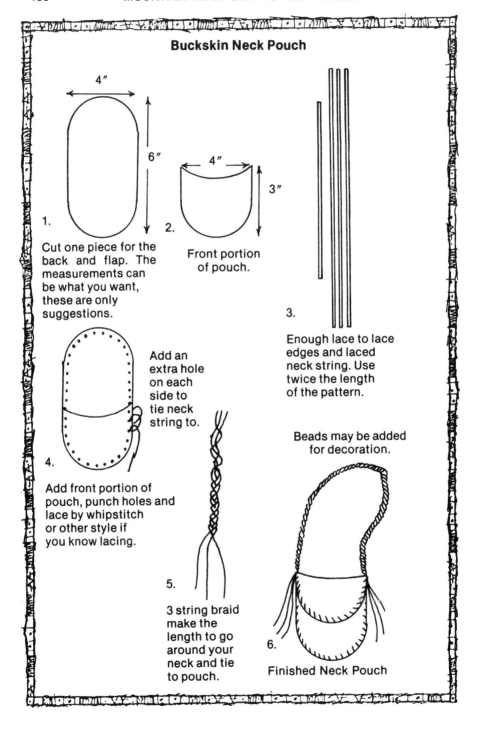

4"

6"

1.

Cut one piece for the back and flap. The measurements can be what you want, these are only suggestions.

4"

3"

2.

Front portion of pouch.

3.

Enough lace to lace edges and laced neck string. Use twice the length of the pattern.

Add an extra hole on each side to tie neck string.

4.

Add front portion of pouch, punch holes and lace by whipstitch or other style if you know lacing.

Beads may be added for decoration.

5.

3 string braid make the length to go around your neck and tie to pouch.

6.

Finished Neck Pouch

Rawhide Bullet Pouch

1.
Use a 4″ × 6″ piece of wet cow rawhide.

2. Cut out two identical shapes with the neck being about ¾″ at the top. Cut out a patch from the excess to make your lace.

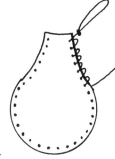

3.
Punch holes with a hole-punch or awl, put both sides together and lace with wet rawhide. Leave a loop on each side on top for ties.

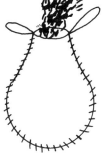

4.
Fill pouch with dry wheat until it bulges and is round. Don't fill with sand or like substance; when it dries, it will be like sand paper if you do.

5.
Make plug out of wood, making the bottom slightly larger than the caliber of ball you are using. Stuff the plug in while the pouch is still wet.

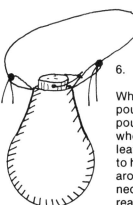

6.
When the pouch is dry, pour out the wheat, add a leather string to hang it around your neck and it's ready to use.

Bullet Pouches

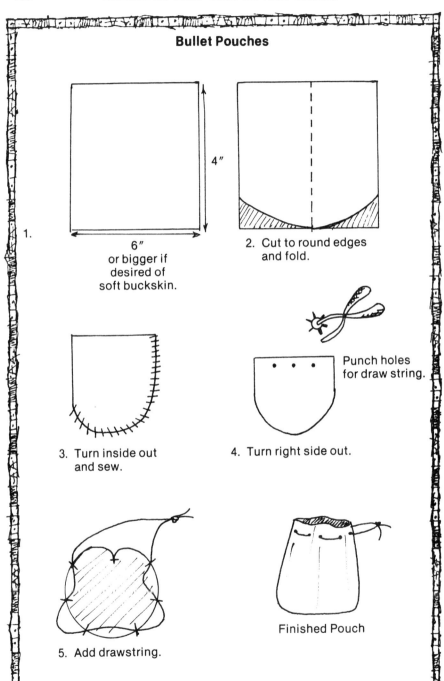

1.

6″
or bigger if
desired of
soft buckskin.

4″

2. Cut to round edges
and fold.

Punch holes
for draw string.

3. Turn inside out
and sew.

4. Turn right side out.

5. Add drawstring.

Finished Pouch

12

Parfleches

These rawhide Indian suitcases were used by the plains Indians for their personal belongings. The rawhide was folded, while still wet, to the desired shape and then dryed under pressure. This type of parflech is good for packing on horses and stacking. The Medicine style parfleck seems to be more easy to manage for getting things in and out. Also, it is decorative either hanging from the dew cloth of a tipi or on the walls of your home.

To obtain the rawhide for these, refer to the chapter on tanning or go to a slaughter house and get a cowhide. Before taking it to the tannery, check to make sure that they make rawhide. The cost is usually $20.00 to $30.00.

When painting them, use a good leather paint obtained at leather craft stores or a good acrylic paint that you buy at paint stores in pint cans.

My medicine style parfleches are constantly in use for carrying my scrimshaw supplies as well as my leather working tools. They are very handy when camping.

If you have a tipi, and it's painted, it could be fun to paint the parfleches to match the colors on the tipi. We did this and it looks sharp.

Parfleche

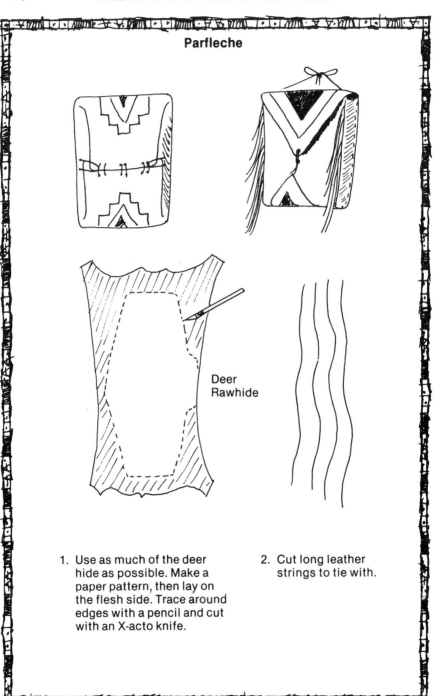

Deer
Rawhide

1. Use as much of the deer
   hide as possible. Make a
   paper pattern, then lay on
   the flesh side. Trace around
   edges with a pencil and cut
   with an X-acto knife.

2. Cut long leather
   strings to tie with.

Parfleches (continued)

3. Take a yard stick and mark as in the diagram on the flesh side.

4. Punch holes with an awl as shown.

5. Soak the rawhide in water until it's flexible, then fold it in on the marks and lay a large flat heavy object on top until dry.

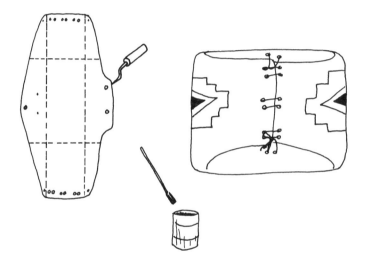

6. Acrylic paint (Acri-vin) and tandy leather paint are the best paints to use.
7. Determine the design you want on a piece of scratch paper, then draw it on the parfleche.
8. Use a brush made for painting acrylics and paint on design.
9. Insert tie strings.

Rawhide Medicine Parfleche

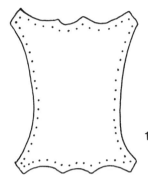

Deerskin rawhide usually works well for this but cowhide can also be used.

1. Cut out a paper template first, using a yardstick. There is no set size, but the bigger, the better.

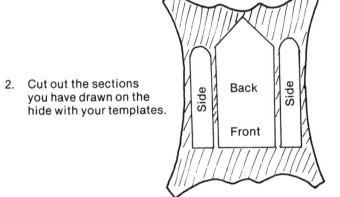

Front
Flap

Side   Back   Side

Front

2. Cut out the sections you have drawn on the hide with your templates.

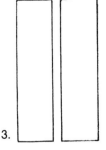

Two strips of soft buckskin the length of the front of the parfleche. The width should be at least 12″.

3.

Fringe Strips

Rawhide Medicine Parfleche (continued)

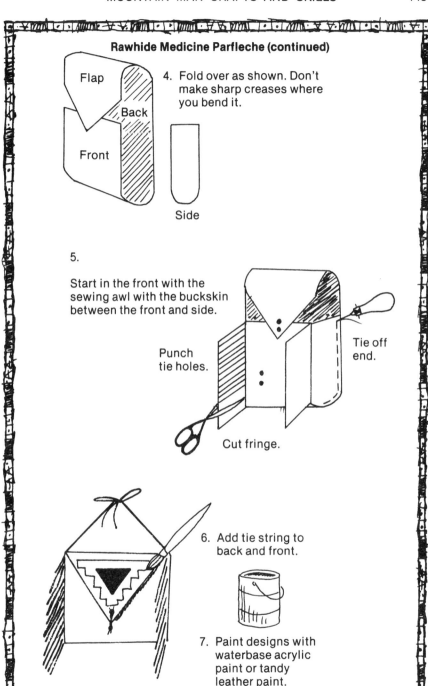

4. Fold over as shown. Don't make sharp creases where you bend it.

5.

Start in the front with the sewing awl with the buckskin between the front and side.

Punch tie holes.

Tie off end.

Cut fringe.

6. Add tie string to back and front.

7. Paint designs with waterbase acrylic paint or tandy leather paint.

13

Scabbards

In order to protect his rifle from the elements and to carry a knife, the trapper used a scabbard.

The type of knife scabbard shown here originated during the Indian wards. The knife sets down into the scabbard with only about 1 inch of the handle showing. The reason for this inaccessibility was self-protection. Prior to the white man's coming, Indians fought each other without really trying to kill. It was enough of an honor to "count coup" on a live opponent. The only problem was that sometimes a warrior was tempted to grab an opponent's exposed knife handle and kill the enemy with his own knife. Therefore, this type of scabbard came into use, which made it almost impossible for someone else to get the knife out. The belt is worn over the front of the scabbard which also held the knife in tight.

To protect your black powder rifle from the elements, a loose fitting scabbard is suggested. It is important not to have an air tight case because any moisture in the rifle will condense and cause rusting. Scabbards were made of leather or excess portions of the blanket from which capote had been made. These blanket coats were worn by both mountain men and Indians.

The tools and materials are shown here and the leather can be scrap for the leather scabbards and the blanket scabbard from the leftovers of the trade blanket.

Knife Scabbard

1.

Rawhide
or
Latigo

Buckskin

2.

The scabbard should be long enough to
allow only about 1″ of the knife handle
to show.

3.

Tools & Supplies
Needed

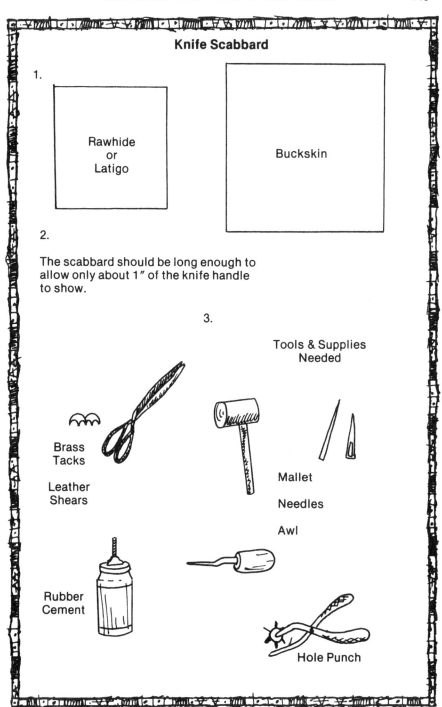

Brass
Tacks

Leather
Shears

Mallet

Needles

Awl

Rubber
Cement

Hole Punch

Knife Scabbard (continued)

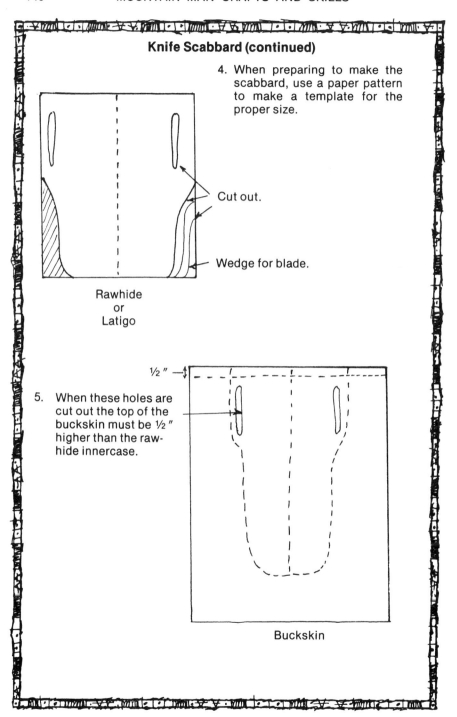

4. When preparing to make the scabbard, use a paper pattern to make a template for the proper size.

Cut out.

Wedge for blade.

Rawhide
or
Latigo

5. When these holes are cut out the top of the buckskin must be ½″ higher than the rawhide innercase.

½″

Buckskin

Knife Scabbard (continued)

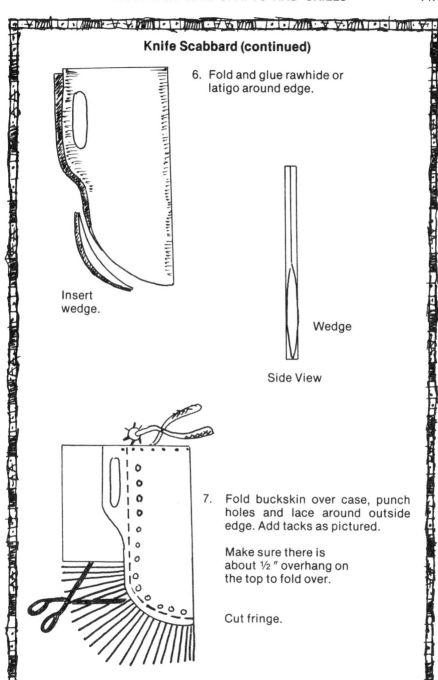

6. Fold and glue rawhide or latigo around edge.

Insert wedge.

Wedge

Side View

7. Fold buckskin over case, punch holes and lace around outside edge. Add tacks as pictured.

Make sure there is about ½ " overhang on the top to fold over.

Cut fringe.

Knife Scabbard (continued)

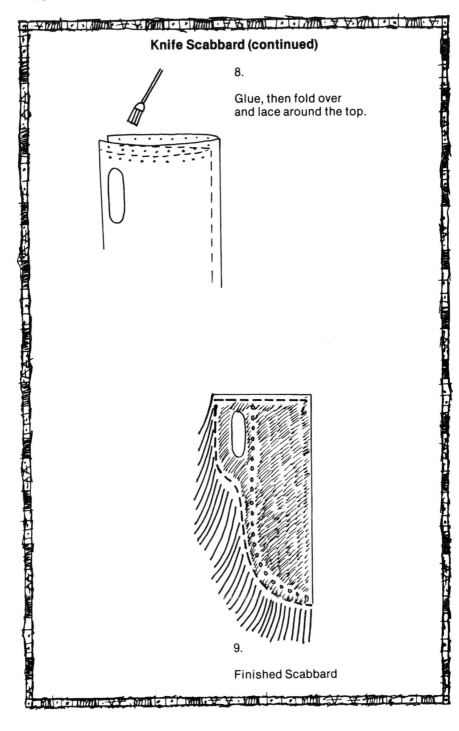

8.

Glue, then fold over
and lace around the top.

9.

Finished Scabbard

Blanket Scabbard

This scabbard is normally used or made after a blanket coat (capote) is sewn and there is excess yardage.

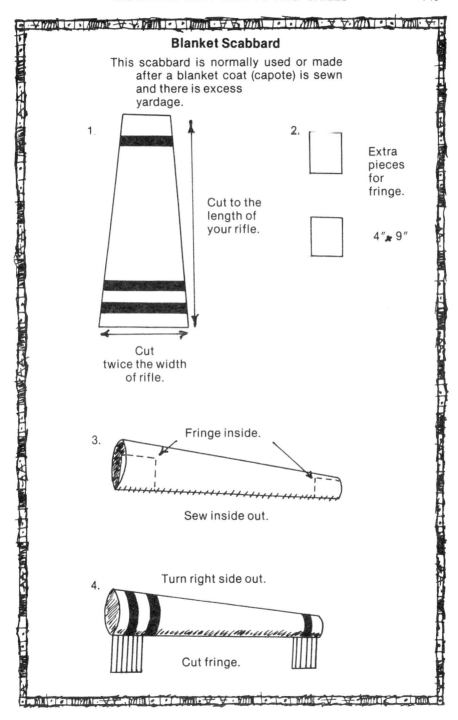

1.

Cut to the length of your rifle.

Cut twice the width of rifle.

2.

Extra pieces for fringe.

4" x 9"

3.

Fringe inside.

Sew inside out.

4.

Turn right side out.

Cut fringe.

Leather Scabbard

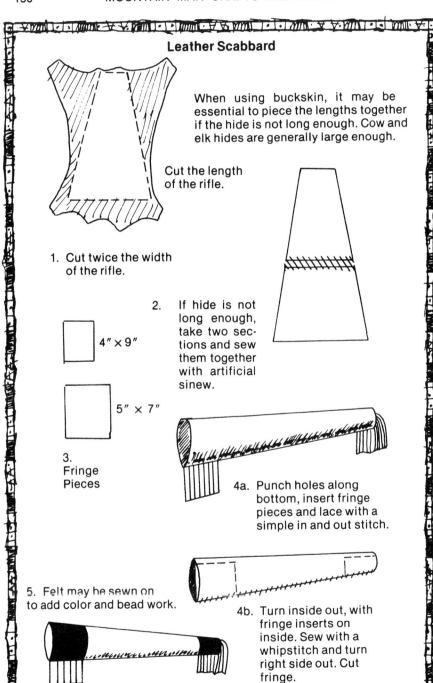

When using buckskin, it may be essential to piece the lengths together if the hide is not long enough. Cow and elk hides are generally large enough.

Cut the length of the rifle.

1. Cut twice the width of the rifle.

2. If hide is not long enough, take two sections and sew them together with artificial sinew.

4" × 9"

5" × 7"

3. Fringe Pieces

4a. Punch holes along bottom, insert fringe pieces and lace with a simple in and out stitch.

5. Felt may be sewn on to add color and bead work.

4b. Turn inside out, with fringe inserts on inside. Sew with a whipstitch and turn right side out. Cut fringe.

14

Beadwork

Prior to the French and British trading with the Indians, beadwork consisted of wampum (trade) belts made of shell. All other work was dyed or done with quills. The white man introduced glass beads to the Indians. From these he made them in strips on a loom for shirts and leggings. For smaller areas, the overlaid and lazy sqaw stitch were useful.

Beads and looms can be purchased at craft stores as well as leather craft stores and sometimes at Indian craft shops. The best way to buy them is by the hank, which is 10 strands of beads on thread for about $1.00 for seed beads. You can either make or buy a loom.

You can bead everything from rosettes for hair and hat pieces, to shirts, dresses, pants, pouches and moccasins.

If you plan to do a lot of hunting in buckskins, it wouldn't be suggested to bead shirts, pants, or moccasins.

Try these methods out and you'll add color and style to your outfit.

Beadwork

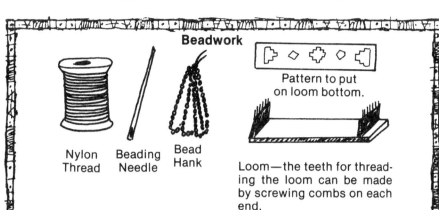

Nylon
Thread

Beading
Needle

Bead
Hank

Pattern to put
on loom bottom.

Loom—the teeth for thread-
ing the loom can be made
by screwing combs on each
end.

Side View
of Strung Loom

Tack
on each
end.

1.

When stringing the loom, make a
double strand on each side for reinforcement. It is also best to make
an odd number of sections so that
a center bead can be established.

Top View
of Strung Loom

2. Make at least 4 runs through
with the beading thread as
shown and tighten together.

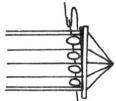

3.
String the amount of beads
required and push them up
under the long strings, wrap
needle and thread around
end and come through top
side of beads. If you missed
one, you will notice because
the bead will sag.

Beadwork (continued)

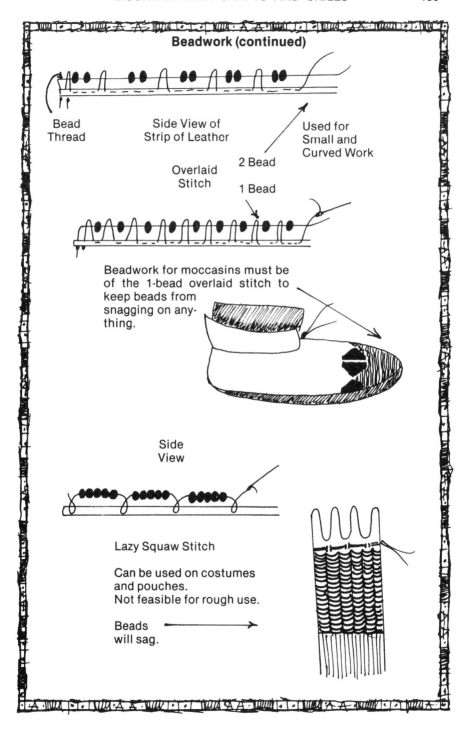

Bead
Thread

Side View of
Strip of Leather

Used for
Small and
Curved Work

Overlaid
Stitch

2 Bead

1 Bead

Beadwork for moccasins must be of the 1-bead overlaid stitch to keep beads from snagging on anything.

Side
View

Lazy Squaw Stitch

Can be used on costumes and pouches.
Not feasible for rough use.

Beads
will sag.

Beadwork (continued)

15

Quillwork

Quillwork was used throughout the continent before beads were introduced and very intricate work was done. Everything from shirts to moccasins were adorned with brightly colored quillwork. The Indians dyed them with natural dyes. Today, Rit dye does the job best.

You cannot buy quills in the store unless you happen to luck out and have a mountain man shop around and they happen to have some. Usually at a Rendezvous where there is a good traders row, someone will have some available for about $.03 apiece.

You need not kill porcupine to get quills. In fact, it's much easier to get them when they're alive and bristle up. That's when you throw your burlap on top of them and pull the quill off.

When you've finished a good piece of work, you'll realize that it took a lot of effort, but the end result will have people wanting you to do it for them.

The wrap is good for pouch fringe decorations and the weave and spot stitch is good for trim on clothing.

Quill Work

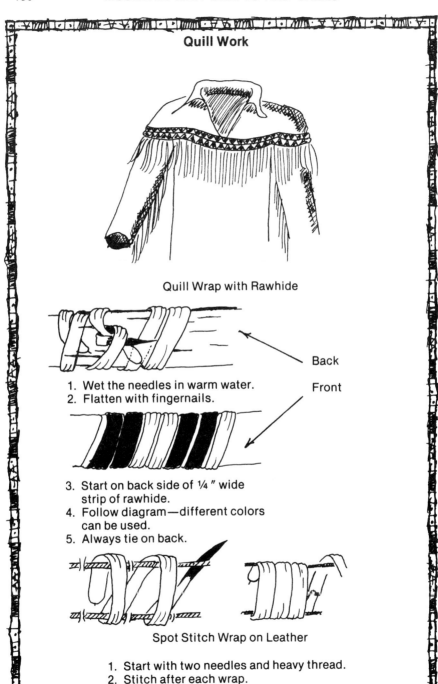

Quill Wrap with Rawhide

Back

Front

1. Wet the needles in warm water.
2. Flatten with fingernails.

3. Start on back side of ¼ " wide
   strip of rawhide.
4. Follow diagram—different colors
   can be used.
5. Always tie on back.

Spot Stitch Wrap on Leather

1. Start with two needles and heavy thread.
2. Stitch after each wrap.

Quillwork (continued)

Quill Weaving

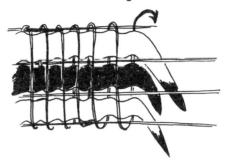

1. Set up loom as if for bead work.

2. Flatten quills but dont soak them in water.

3. Take the thread with the arrowhead on diagram and go over and under the quills as you fold the quills down, then up.

Double Wrap on Leather

1. Spot stitch after each wrap.

2. Follow diagram except make stitches as close to quill as possible.

3. When finished, it should look like this—a very tight fold.

Picking & Dyeing Porcupine Quills

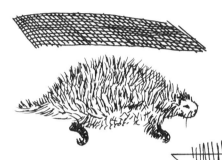

1. Since some states protect the porcupine, make sure you know your state's laws on killing them.
2. If the law says you may shoot them, you can use the claws for necklaces, guard hair for roaches and quills for decoration.

3. Take a burlap sack and put on top of the porcupine (works better when it is alive), push down, then pull off.

4. Pull quills through the burlap.

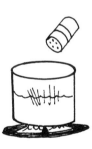

5. Take a gallon can, fill half with water. Put some powdered cleanser in and stir. While water is heating, add quills; stir and rinse. This will degrease quills.

6. Add ½ gal. clean water then add ¼ bottle Rit liquid dye (whatever color you desire). Heat.

Picking & Dyeing Porcupine Quills (continued)

7. Add 1 teaspoon of sugar.
   This sets the dye in the
   quills.

8. Add quills and stir
   every few minutes until
   desired color is reached.

9. Store quills in
   containers with lids.

16

Firemaking

Naturally a match is the easiest way to start a fire, but there may be times when you may not have one around and you definitely don't want to be seen striking one at a Rendezvous. For survival purposes, the bow drill can be a life saver. Your bootlace and knife are all the equipment you need to carry because nature can supply the rest of the needed materials. It requires skill to start a fire with a bow drill, so it is a good idea to practice this skill before it becomes essential.

Flint and steel is generally the mountain man's fire starter. It requires some type of container and a pouch for the needed materials. As with the bow drill, learning how to use the materials is essential. Fire making is an event of the mountain man run contest at Rendezvous time, so if you plan to compete, be prepared.

The steel can be purchased at some Black Powder Shops or at a Rendezvous. If you know how to work with high carbon steel (such as files), you can make your own. The temper must be such that, when finished, it will strike a spark on flint.

Flint can be found in rocky country and is easy to get. My son always comes back from camping trips with a pocketful of flint.

When making the charred cloth, cut up pure cotton that is not permanent press. Put it in a can with a lid that has small holes punched in the top. Lay it on a fire, taking it off after ½ hour or so. Let it cool, then take out the cloth and put it in your container.

People seem to be amazed when they find that someone can do this, and it is self-satisfying to know it works.

160

Fire Making

1. Octagonal Stick
   Pointed on Top
   Rounded on Bottom

2. Hand block of hardwood
   with smooth cupped hole.

3. Bow made of stiff
   branch arms length.

   Boot lace for
   string.

4. Fireboard, make
   shallow hole with V
   to catch ember.

5. Foil or heavy
   paper to catch
   ember.

6. Tinder made into
   nest of cedar or
   sage bark.

7.

Place fireboard over foil. Twist bowstring
around spindle so bow is tight. Put blunt end
down on spindle, place block on point, set in
hole, holding block against knee. Start with
long strokes, increasing the pressure.

Fire Making (continued)

Until heavy smoke appears, take board and check for spark. If a glow appears, set it in the tinder and blow upward gently until it breaks into flame.

Flint & Steel

1. Steel   2. Charred   3. Flint
                Cloth

4. Nest of   5. Small, dry
   tinder made   twigs.
   with cedar or
   sagebrush bark.

6. Place charred cloth on
   top of flint with edge of
   cloth next to edge of
   flint. Strike downward
   quickly with steel and
   continue until cloth
   catches spark.

Fire Making (continued)

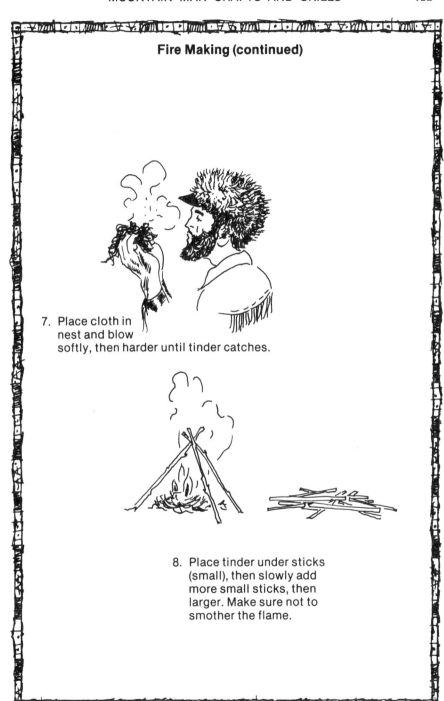

7. Place cloth in nest and blow softly, then harder until tinder catches.

8. Place tinder under sticks (small), then slowly add more small sticks, then larger. Make sure not to smother the flame.

17

The
Tipi

The mountain man of the past lived in anything considered a shelter from snow caves in the winter, to lean-tos or tipis or small cabins if he was lucky. They were constantly on the move during the trapping season and always in search of new areas for fur, so a cabin was out of the question for most of the time. The lean-to was his home while trapping, although many times he would live in a tipi when staying with the plains Indians.

Today the mountain man enjoys the comfort of the tipi and you'll find some sharp looking ones in the tipi villages during rendezvous. Even today with modern technology man hasn't equaled the tip for camping comfort as far as tents go. In fact a neighbor gave up on his camper he was building after having camped in a tipi with us, and got one himself. For man, who are concerned with survival and storage for emergencies, a tipi can be considered as an emergency home which could be quite comfortable. The tipi offers walking space, with plenty of head room, cooking facilities, air conditioning, warmth, storage and privacy.

Making the tip looks harder than it is. A good straight stitch sewing machine on the kitchen table and a driveway for laying it out for measurement are the basic necessities for the construction. The best weight canvas is 10 oz. in a 72″ width although 36″ width can be used as well. Canvas can be ordered through various distributors. Waterproofing can be done with a sprayer using a product called Swan Coat available at laundry supply distributors. The cover and door flap take 40 yards of canvas, and the dew cloth (liner) requires 17 yards of muslin of 72″ width. Use of a good heavy rot resistant thread sold at tent and awning stores.

Other items needed are 15 feet of twill tape for door flap ties; 30 feet of ½ ″ rope for tieing down the tipi poles; 300 feet of ¼ ″ nylon cord for ties on the cover and liner; and another 45′ ¼ ″ rope for the liner rope. Also you will need to make about 25 pegs of some hardwood about 15″ in length to use as stakes; about twelve 12″ long lacing pins made from elm or other wood. Ten is all that is needed but it is wise to have extra. One last item is the rain pegs. These are small dowels 2″ long, about ¼ ″ in size which go between the liner ties and the poles to keep rain from dripping from the liner. About 40 of these are needed.

Tipi Construction

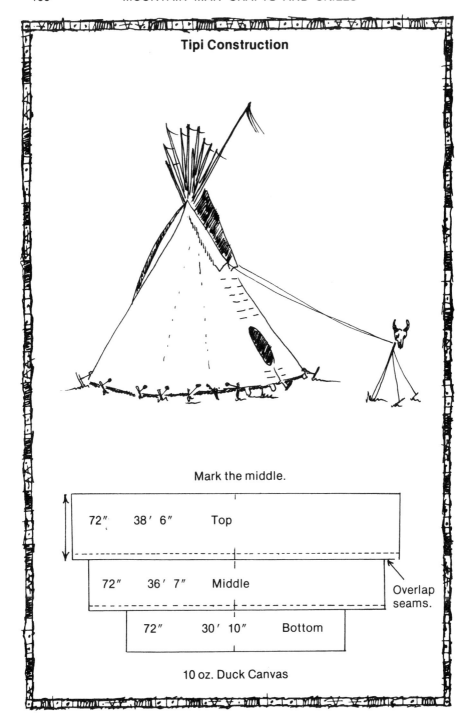

Mark the middle.

72″	38′ 6″	Top
72″	36′ 7″	Middle
72″	30′ 10″	Bottom

Overlap seams.

10 oz. Duck Canvas

Tipi Construction (continued)

Top Strip

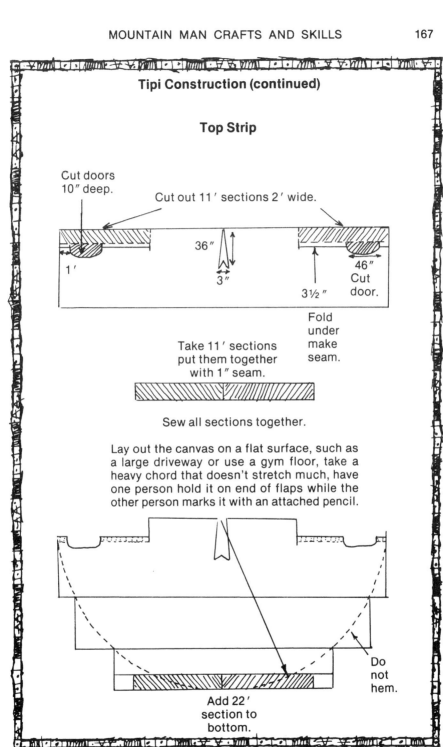

Cut doors 10″ deep.

Cut out 11′ sections 2′ wide.

36″

3″

1′

46″
Cut door.

3½″

Fold under make seam.

Take 11′ sections put them together with 1″ seam.

Sew all sections together.

Lay out the canvas on a flat surface, such as a large driveway or use a gym floor, take a heavy chord that doesn't stretch much, have one person hold it on end of flaps while the other person marks it with an attached pencil.

Do not hem.

Add 22′ section to bottom.

Tipi Construction (continued)

Use 2 nylon twill tapes
3½′ long; fold them as
shown on inside of canvas.
Sew for reinforcement by
sewing across and up on
tab. The ties should be
3′ long.

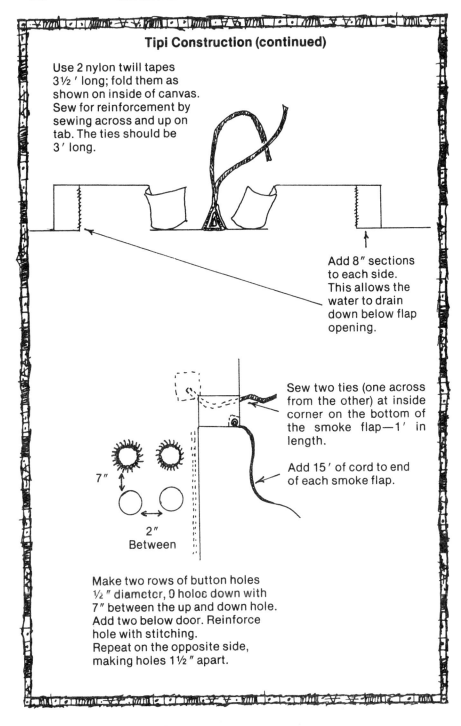

Add 8″ sections
to each side.
This allows the
water to drain
down below flap
opening.

Sew two ties (one across
from the other) at inside
corner on the bottom of
the smoke flap—1′ in
length.

Add 15′ of cord to end
of each smoke flap.

7″

2″
Between

Make two rows of button holes
½″ diameter, 0 holes down with
7″ between the up and down hole.
Add two below door. Reinforce
hole with stitching.
Repeat on the opposite side,
making holes 1½″ apart.

Smoke Flap Pole Pocket

Use an 8″ section by 5½″ of canvas. Taper to top at 3″, fold over and double stitch. Sew cup so the pocket is on the outside of the top flap. Reinforce sewing to the flap. These pockets must take a lot of pressure.

One on the upper outside of each smoke flap.

Door Flap

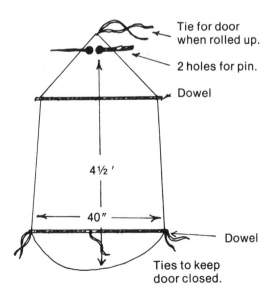

Tie for door when rolled up.

2 holes for pin.

Dowel

4½′

40″

Dowel

Ties to keep door closed.

Dewcloth Liner

Your tipi will not function properly without this liner!

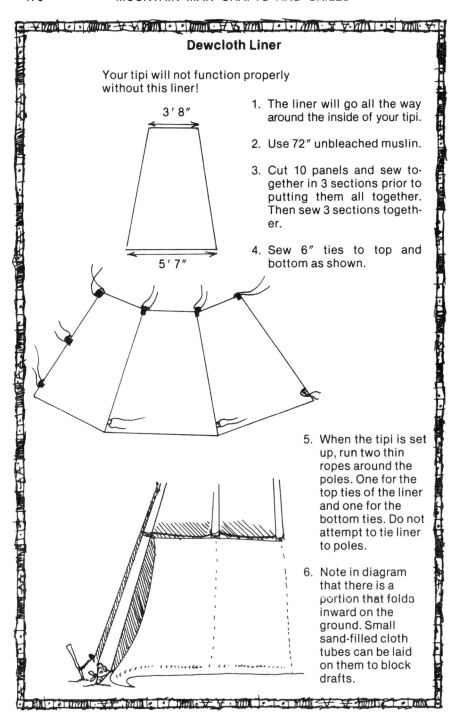

3' 8"

5' 7"

1. The liner will go all the way around the inside of your tipi.

2. Use 72" unbleached muslin.

3. Cut 10 panels and sew together in 3 sections prior to putting them all together. Then sew 3 sections together.

4. Sew 6" ties to top and bottom as shown.

5. When the tipi is set up, run two thin ropes around the poles. One for the top ties of the liner and one for the bottom ties. Do not attempt to tie liner to poles.

6. Note in diagram that there is a portion that folds inward on the ground. Small sand-filled cloth tubes can be laid on them to block drafts.

Ozan

The ozan acts as an inner roof
and will help retain heat, plus give
you some privacy when wanted.

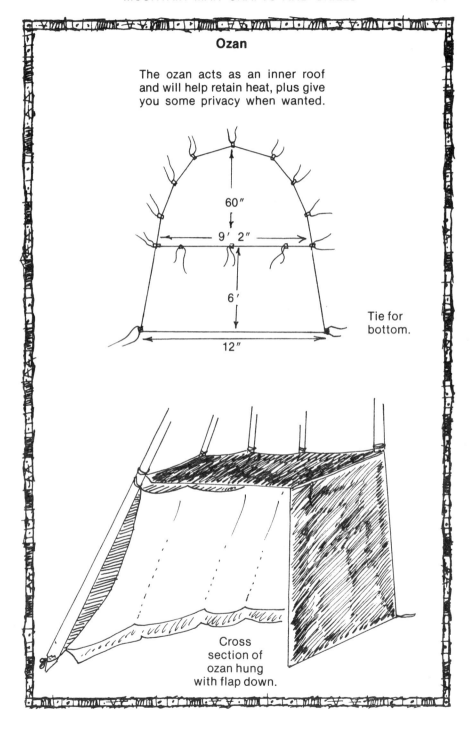

60"

9' 2"

6'

12"

Tie for
bottom.

Cross
section of
ozan hung
with flap down.

Setting Up the Tipi

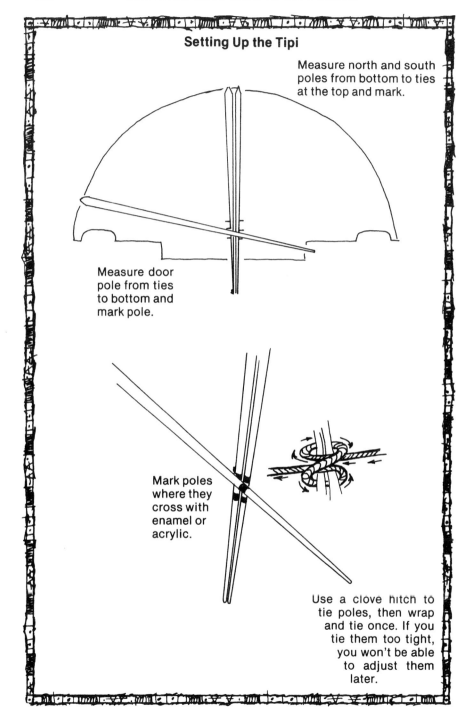

Measure north and south poles from bottom to ties at the top and mark.

Measure door pole from ties to bottom and mark pole.

Mark poles where they cross with enamel or acrylic.

Use a clove hitch to tie poles, then wrap and tie once. If you tie them too tight, you won't be able to adjust them later.

Setting Up the Tipi (continued)

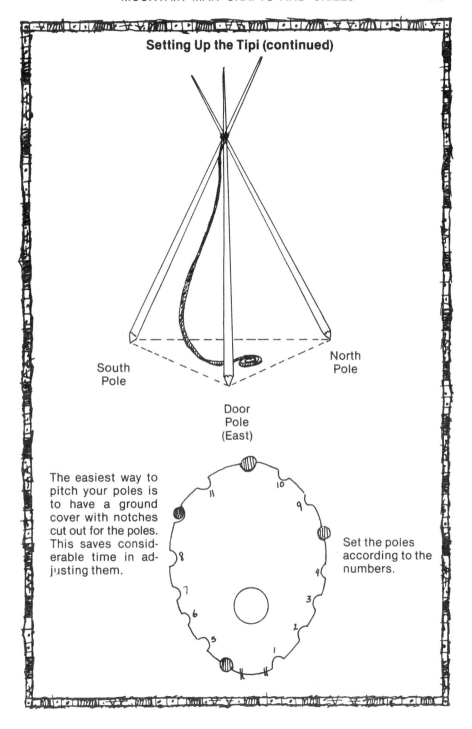

South
Pole

North
Pole

Door
Pole
(East)

The easiest way to pitch your poles is to have a ground cover with notches cut out for the poles. This saves considerable time in adjusting them.

Set the poles according to the numbers.

Setting Up the Tipi (continued)

Once the poles are tied down, tie the top of the tipi to the mark on the lift pole. If someone is helping, have them put their foot on the bottom while you lift. Otherwise, put a heavy rock at the base to keep it from sliding while lifting.

After the 14 poles are pitched, take the rope and wrap around about 3 times, bring through and tie down tightly.

Cross
stakes
for
tying
tipi
down.

Setting Up the Tipi (continued)

For the ties on the cover, insert a round
rock and tie nylon chord around leaving
plenty for twisting rope and tying down
on the stake.

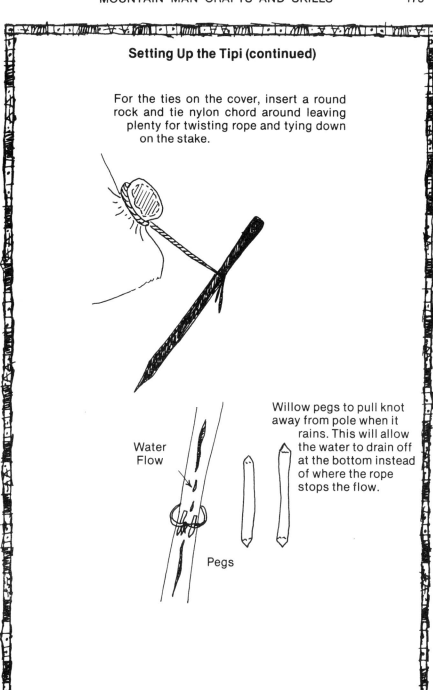

Water
Flow

Pegs

Willow pegs to pull knot
away from pole when it
rains. This will allow
the water to drain off
at the bottom instead
of where the rope
stops the flow.

Setting Up the Tipi (continued)

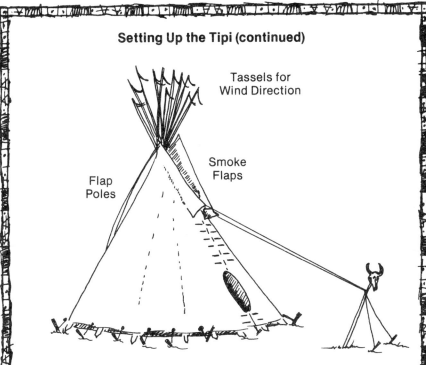

The tipi should have more slant to the front than the back. Pitch with door to the east in most instances.

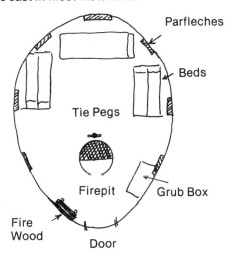

Setting Up the Tipi (continued)

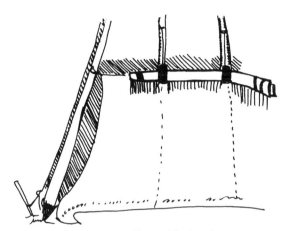

Hang rifle in slings
from poles.

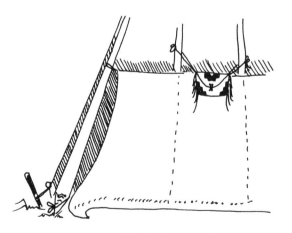

Parfleches can be
hung between poles.

Stripping Poles

1. The best type of tipi pole is lodge pole pine.

2. The base of the pole should be 2½ " to 3" thick and 25 ' long.

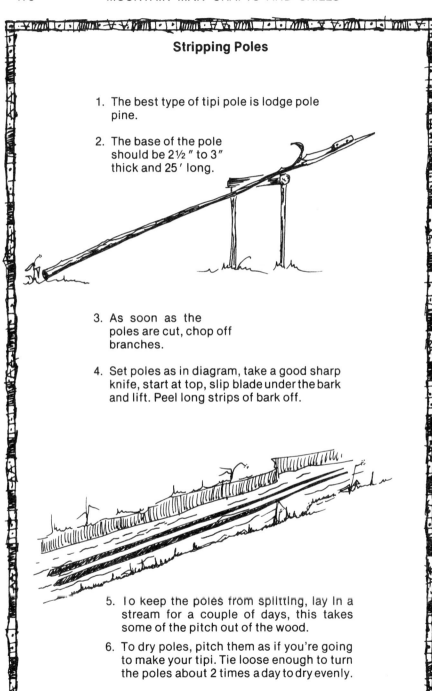

3. As soon as the poles are cut, chop off branches.

4. Set poles as in diagram, take a good sharp knife, start at top, slip blade under the bark and lift. Peel long strips of bark off.

5. To keep the poles from splitting, lay in a stream for a couple of days, this takes some of the pitch out of the wood.

6. To dry poles, pitch them as if you're going to make your tipi. Tie loose enough to turn the poles about 2 times a day to dry evenly.

Tipi Pole Racks

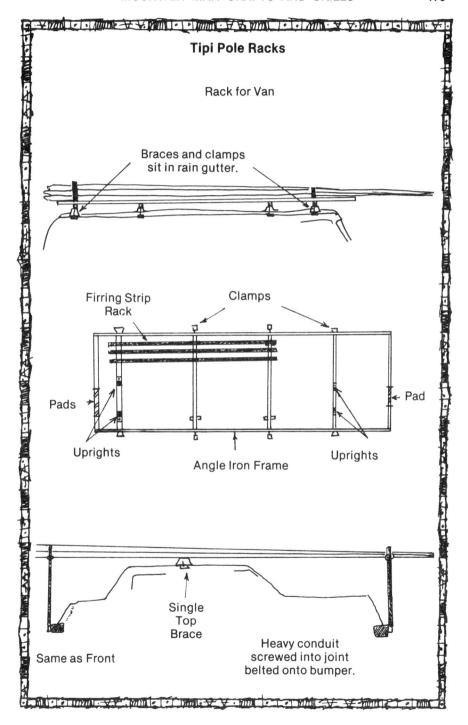

Rack for Van

Braces and clamps
sit in rain gutter.

Firring Strip
Rack

Clamps

Pads

Pad

Uprights

Angle Iron Frame

Uprights

Single
Top
Brace

Same as Front

Heavy conduit
screwed into joint
belted onto bumper.

Latrine

When camping in your tipi, it is usually for several days or more. Build a latrine a good 50 to 100 yards away from the campsite. Use 3 poles or trees to stretch a canvas tarp on. Build a triangle seat sturdy enough to hold an adult. Dig a hole at least 2′ deep. Keep lime bag next to dirt pile. Use a small amount of lime with dirt. It will decompose matter.

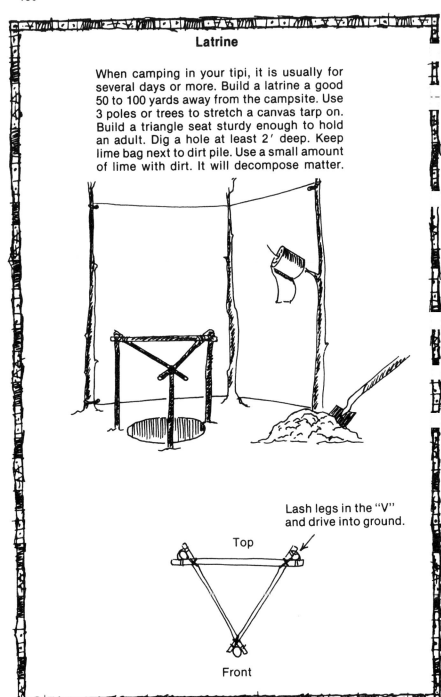

Lash legs in the "V" and drive into ground.

Top

Front

Fire Pits For the Tipi

One of the best features of a tipi is the fact that it is made to have a fire inside. When camping in your tipi it is essential to be aware of the laws concerning fire building in the area. Some areas, such as the tipi village at the Fort Bridger, Wyoming Rendezvous, will not allow fires to be built on the ground so an alternative must be used. A metal fire pit can serve this purpose. It also has the advantage of being portable and easier to use for cooking. The metal will also radiate heat and serve as a stove. As with all fires caution needs to be taken when children are around.

When camping in the wilderness, a pit can be dug towards the front of the tipi which allows the smoke to clear quicker and gives more living space to the rear of the tipi. If the camps is to be more permanent than a few days you may wish to build a fire vent. Dig a trench large enough and deep enough for a four inch stove pipe. This will go from the fire pit under the floor out to the outside of the tipi. This will allow adequate air to get under the fire and prevent it from getting smoky. Also, a word of caution, if you have the tipi pitched and it gets snowed on, be sure to clear the snow from around the outside bottom edge so that air can get in to draw the smoke up, or if you have the fire vent set up, be sure no snow blocks the pipe opening outside.

Tipi Fire Pit

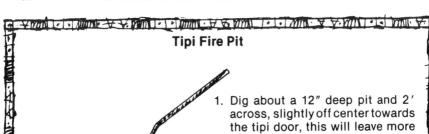

1. Dig about a 12″ deep pit and 2′ across, slightly off center towards the tipi door, this will leave more living room towards the back.

2. Line pit with flat rocks if possible and stack two high around edge. Make sure rocks are stable enough to support weight.

3. Top View. Rocks will retain some heat during the night.

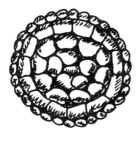

4. If you plan to do some winter camping where snow is possible rig up a 4″ stove pipe to run under the floor and outside as pictured.

Tripod
for
Cooking

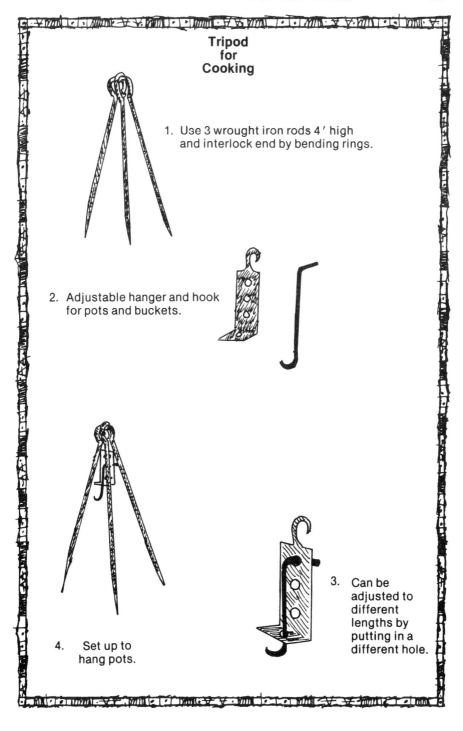

1. Use 3 wrought iron rods 4′ high and interlock end by bending rings.

2. Adjustable hanger and hook for pots and buckets.

3. Can be adjusted to different lengths by putting in a different hole.

4. Set up to hang pots.

Metal Tipi Fire Pit

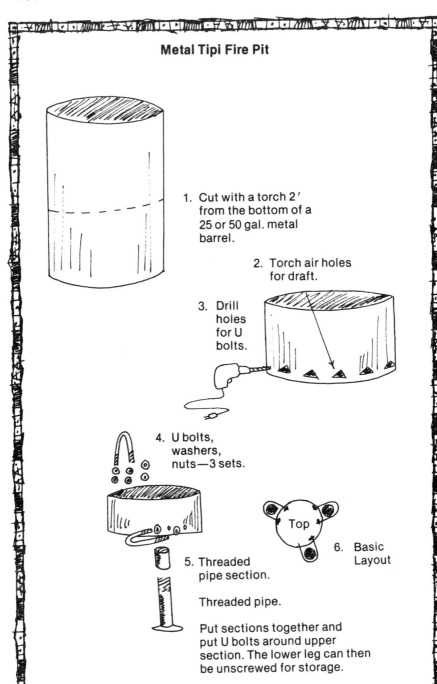

1. Cut with a torch 2′ from the bottom of a 25 or 50 gal. metal barrel.

2. Torch air holes for draft.

3. Drill holes for U bolts.

4. U bolts, washers, nuts—3 sets.

5. Threaded pipe section.

6. Basic Layout

Top

Threaded pipe.

Put sections together and put U bolts around upper section. The lower leg can then be unscrewed for storage.

Metal Tipi Fire Pit (continued)

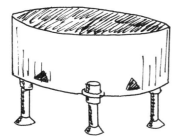

7. Side View

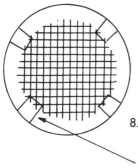

8. Sections of angle iron can be welded to the inside about 4" up from the bottom to support expanded steel screen which will keep the bottom from burning out.

9. Fire to be built on screen.

Dirt can be added to bottom to insulate.

Firepit Accessories

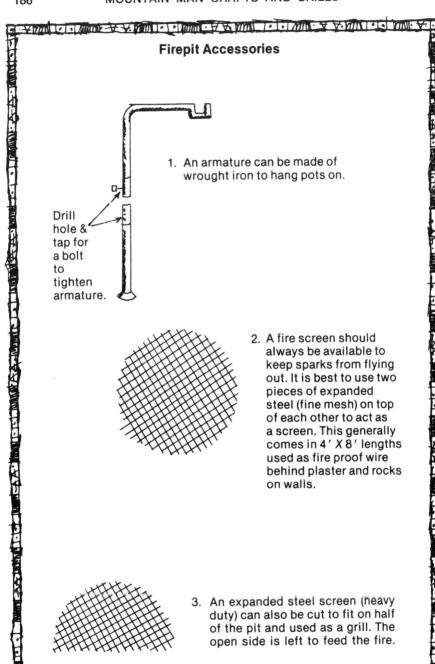

1. An armature can be made of wrought iron to hang pots on.

Drill hole & tap for a bolt to tighten armature.

2. A fire screen should always be available to keep sparks from flying out. It is best to use two pieces of expanded steel (fine mesh) on top of each other to act as a screen. This generally comes in 4' X 8' lengths used as fire proof wire behind plaster and rocks on walls.

3. An expanded steel screen (heavy duty) can also be cut to fit on half of the pit and used as a grill. The open side is left to feed the fire.

The Tipi

As you can see, there is a lot that goes into the construction of a tipi. If you are planning just an overnighter, it might save you a lot of headaches to just throw a regular tent in the back of your vehicle. The tipi is made for extended camping trips when you want to set up for several days.

You'll find the more times you set up the tipi, the more adept you become and it will go up faster with more ease.

As of this writing, a new acquaintance from South Dakota came to Utah to pick up a tipi and visit relatives. We had a 4th of July Rendezvous with our club and as usual this year, it rained. He camped in a tipi and sent back to South Dakota a changed person all set to do the whole mountain man bit.

It's amazing what happens when your neighborhood finds out that you have one, so don't be surprised if you start seeing tipi poles in neighbor's back yards. It happens!

18

Baker's Tent and Snow Cave

This particular tent is very popular with Rendezvous traders. It doesn't take up as much room as a tipi and the trapper's goods can be set on display and still be shaded from the sun and protected from the weather. This is an excellent tent for an over-nighter when you still want to be primitive, such as in a rendezvous setting. A small reflector fire can be built under the flap without damaging it and this will warm the interior a great deal.

We tested this tent, which my wife made, on a windy, rainy day with it pitched away from the wind. We sat in our shirt sleeves and were very comfortable. That night about 2:00 a.m., we noticed, to our dismay, a slight sag on the top. We looked outside and found more than a foot of snow had accumulated. We shoveled off this layer of snow, fearing that the tent could not support the weight. By morning there was 21″ on the ground. We estimated that we had 1,100 pounds of wet snow on the top of the tent and felt fortunate that the pole lashings and a good sewing job had prevented what could have been a bad experience.

When pitching the tent, lash the three front poles, then the three back poles, then the two poles on each side. Tie the back of the tent first and stake down the lines in the back. Then tie the front and then the sides. Stake down the ties around the bottom. It is always nice, if possible, to have a ground cloth to keep the area clean and dry.

The directions on the following pages explain how much material you will need.

You can obtain your canvas at tent and awning supply stores and your poles will have to be cut from Lodge Pole Pine or a similar straight, round wood.

Build your fire (a small reflector type) right in front of the front with the overhand above it. It won't burn the top flap as long as the fire is small enough.

When not even a Baker's tent or long enough poles for a lean-to are available, a snow cave can be quite comfortable when there is a breeze. Naturally you must have snow deep enough to build one.

Bakers Tent

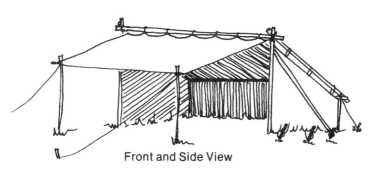

Front and Side View

1. Use 72″, 10 oz. canvas.
2. 16 yards length.
3. Enough cord for ties.
4. 4 poles for front, 2 for top,
   2 for back, and 2 for sides.

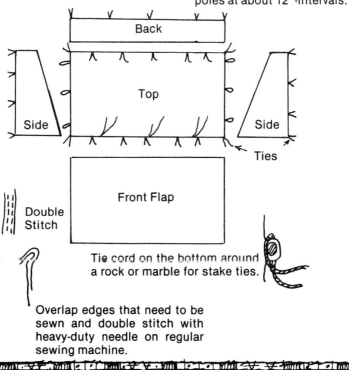

Sew cord to top for ties on poles at about 12″-intervals.

Back

Side

Top

Side

Ties

Double Stitch

Front Flap

Tie cord on the bottom around a rock or marble for stake ties.

Overlap edges that need to be sewn and double stitch with heavy-duty needle on regular sewing machine.

Snow Cave

The snow cave can be made out of a snow drift hollowed out for a couple of individuals. It takes considerable work to do this, but survival may make it necessary. Start low on the drift, dig in, then up. Follow the diagram.

Caution:

Snow caves are not to be considered as permanent shelters, but for temporary, one-night occupancy, to protect one from the elements. In a long-term situation, snow caves deteriorate from the warm air inside and can collapse. If possible, choose a north slope, out of the sun, or build in shaded areas to prevent major shrinkage.

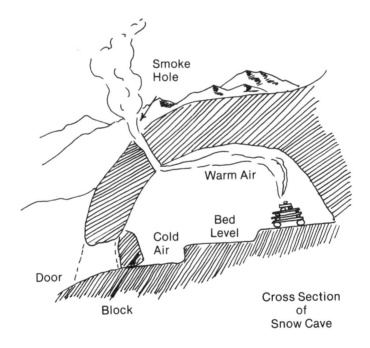

Smoke Hole

Warm Air

Bed Level

Cold Air

Door

Block

Cross Section of Snow Cave

19

Willow
Backrest
Chair

The Indians used willow chairs in their tipis as a backrest and are very convenient for modern use because they are easily portable. Our modern folding chairs are also nice, but they don't exactly fit the tipi atmosphere. When choosing willows for your chair, it is important to find the type of willow illustrated on the left. They grow in large, dense stands but not in single clumps. Cut the willow at the base and strip the bark off the same day for a smoother surface. You may want to leave the bark on for design purposes, however, the stripped willows make a prettier chair. Assemble the chair after the sticks have had sufficient time to dry. It is also necessary to trim off the knobs left from the branch joints after they have dried.

The tripod poles are made from the tips of lodgepole pine; other similar woods do as well, as long as it has the strength to hold when you put your backrest on it and lean back.

The Indians would also take two 6′ poles that are 3″-4″ around, lay them down and stake them wide enough apart to lay the back rest on full length and use it as their bed by laying furs on it for cushion and it would keep them off the damp ground. This also got rid of any little rock spots that can cause misery when trying to sleep.

You may want to make them smaller. If so, just reduce the size to fit your convenience. Once you've got the sticks peeled, dried, and trimmed, the rest is easy and quick, taking only about a day to complete.

Willow Back Rest Chair

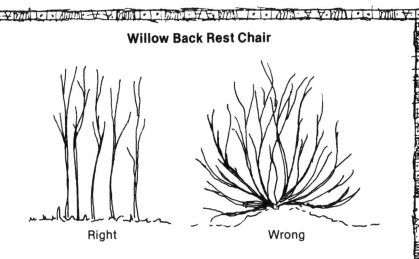

Right   Wrong

1.

After stripping the bark, immediately after cutting, tie sticks in small, tight bundles to keep them from warping.

2. Set up to make in the field.

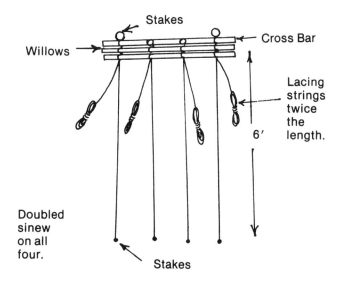

Stakes

Willows

Cross Bar

Lacing strings twice the length.

6'

Doubled sinew on all four.

Stakes

Willow Back Rest Chair (continued)

3. Place each willow with a thick end next to a small end.

Place the willow under the stretched string, then the loose cord is tied to the first willow and pulled down, then up around the willow, over the top of the top cord and down between the willow. Repeat until finished.

4. If you plan to make a number of back rests at home, a framed setup may work best using 1″ firring strips.

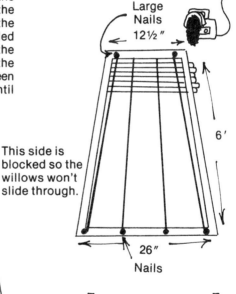

Trim off with hand or electric saw.

Large Nails

← 12½″ →

6′

This side is blocked so the willows won't slide through.

← 26″ →

Nails

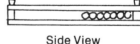

Side View

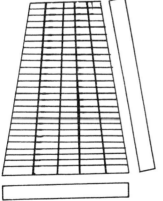

5.

Add wool trim around edge.

Fold and sew.

Willow Back Rest Chair (continued)

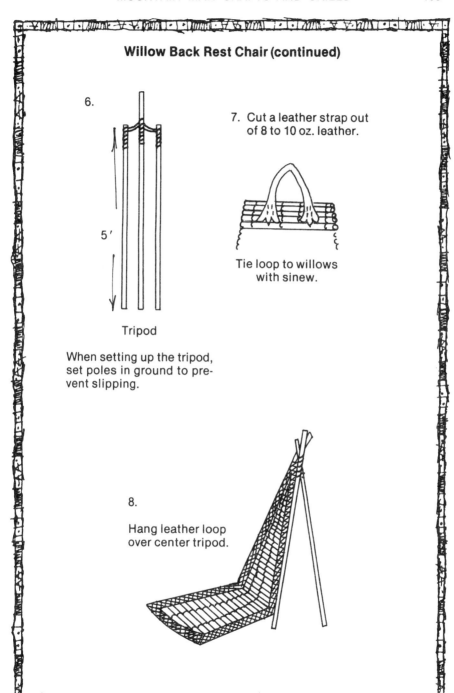

6.

5'

Tripod

7. Cut a leather strap out of 8 to 10 oz. leather.

Tie loop to willows with sinew.

When setting up the tripod, set poles in ground to prevent slipping.

8.

Hang leather loop over center tripod.

20

Trade
Box

The trade box or cassette as it was sometimes called was well used during the fur trade era by the French-Canadians, Hudson's Bay Company and the American Fur Company, then later by others. This was a water-tight pine trunk used for holding the goods to be traded for furs.

The trade box shown here is somewhat different in style so that you may use not only trade goods in them, but also store buckskins. They were also sturdy enough to stand or sit on. As a matter of fact, they make nice, temporary seats in the tipi.

Any type of wood may be used, preferable pine, because it is so much lighter than hardwood. Mine are made of solid oak and are very heavy to lift when full.

For actual replicas of the original style cassette, contact

Harvey F. Wood
3121 South 8th East
Salt Lako City, Utah 84106

He has researched these and makes them with dovetailing, grooving, and Japanned lifting handles. He charges from $125.00 to $200.00 depending on the size of the box.

If you have some basic carpentry skills, this box should not be too hard and will give you many years of fine use.

Trade Box

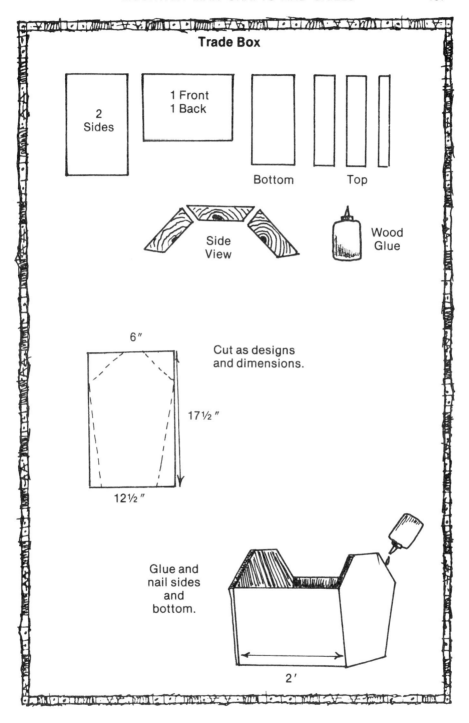

2 Sides

1 Front
1 Back

Bottom   Top

Side View

Wood Glue

6″

Cut as designs and dimensions.

17½″

12½″

Glue and nail sides and bottom.

2′

Trade Box (continued)

Glue and nail
3 top sections.

Torch wood, sand and
cut around
to make lid.

12¼ "

Add hinges and
leather handles.

Two leather
strips cut
for locks.

Thread arrow tip
through hole
that is brought
up through
top loop.

Trade Box (continued)

Basic Finished
Box

An addition to
the box can
be a tray.

2 strips to hold
tray on inside of box

Front of Box

2 Pieces
Front & Back

2
Sides

Bottom

Finished Tray

21
Grub
Box

It is a good idea to have some type of a sturdy container for your food and cooking gear when camping. Eventually card board boxes fall apart and it can be quite a headache when the bottom falls out.

This is just one idea that can be used. The information contained here is minimal, and the bracework on the inside of the box is not shown, but corners, and below each drawer, need braces made of 1" × 2" pine for sliding and reinforcement.

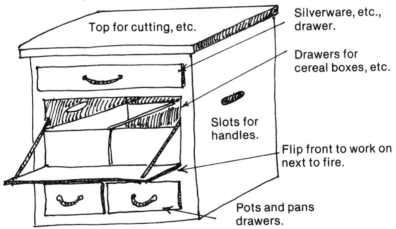

Top for cutting, etc.

Silverware, etc., drawer.

Drawers for cereal boxes, etc.

Slots for handles.

Flip front to work on next to fire.

Pots and pans drawers.

If you know very little about carpentry, pass this one up or find someone that can build it for you.

Any size or shape can be made to suit your individual needs. The one illustrated here serves a family of seven adequately for several days. The top is heavy and can take punishment. The top drawer is used for first aid equipment, cutlery, and other small items. The middle drawers can be used for boxed items or larger bottles, as there is adequate room to set them upright. The lower drawers are tall enough for a mason jar and large enough for a large cast iron griddle to set flat on the bottom. The drop leaf table is used for additional work surface when cooking on the lodge fire.

Grub Box (continued)

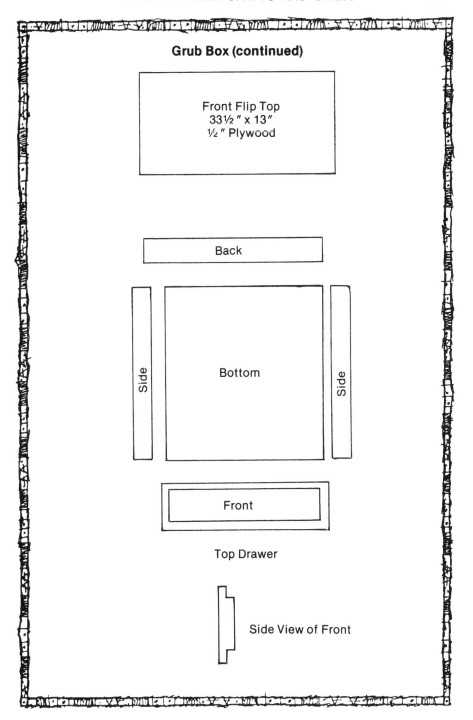

Front Flip Top
33½″ x 13″
½″ Plywood

Back

Side

Bottom

Side

Front

Top Drawer

Side View of Front

Grub Box (continued)

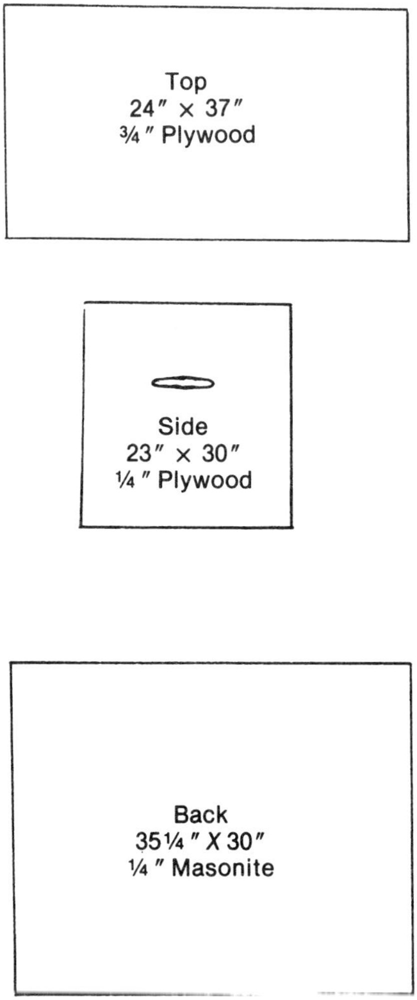

Top
24″ × 37″
¾″ Plywood

Side
23″ × 30″
¼″ Plywood

Back
35¼″ X 30″
¼″ Masonite

Grub Box (continued)

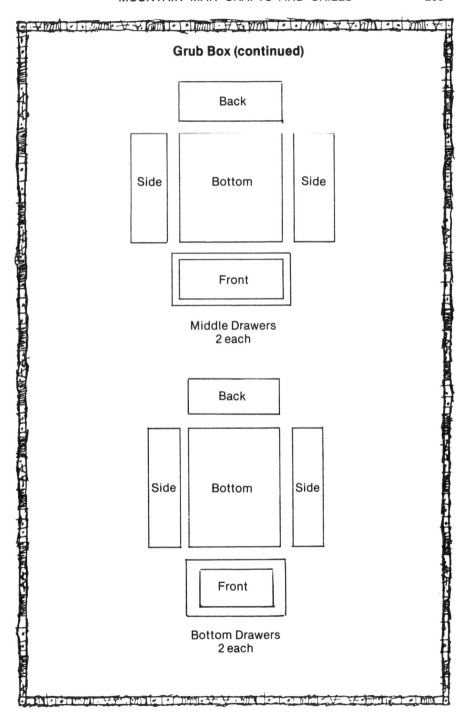

Middle Drawers
2 each

Bottom Drawers
2 each

22

Eating Utensils and Cookware

Not all mountain men were of low calibre and ate with just their fingers, although it was common to do so when among the Indians.

At the forts, china from England appeared as well as some nice silverware. At the Fur Trade Museum in the Teton National Park in Wyoming, there are examples of eating and cooking utensils actually used by the trappers.

Shown here are examples of some primitive, yet good, useable items—a basic knife, fork, and spoon made of small rod steel and horn for a spoon. These styles can be purchased at Rendezvous and Black Powder shops; or, if you have the equipment, you can make them yourself as shown in this chapter.

Plates made of tin, covered with baked enamel, serve for family purposes, or be industrious and make some wooden bowls. Cups can be made of tin or cow horn.

Cooking pots of cast-iron are best for cooking over a fire along with a tin frying pan, but high-fire stoneware (clay) casseroles can be used for pit baking.

It is unique to see a family at Rendezvous eating with mountain man style utensils and it lends greatly to the atmosphere of the occasion.

Steel Knife, Fork & Spoons

Steel Knife, twisted handle,
forged blade.

Steel Fork, twisted handle.

Steel Spoon, twisted handle,
forged.

Horn Spoon

Eating Utensils

Tin Plate

Wooden Bowl

Tin Cup

Horn Cup

Cookware

Stoneware Pot

Cast Iron
Dutch Oven

Tin Frying Pan

Forging
A
Knife

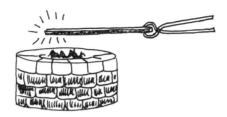

Heat steel rod 8″ long until cherry red.

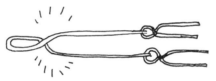

While hot, twist until ends meet.

Flatten a piece of rolled steel for knife blade.

Place blade between handle while both are cherry red hot, solder with powdered flax and weld with hammer blows on anvil.

Forging A Knife (continued)

Cool in water.

Sharpen blade
on grinder.

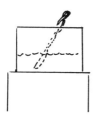

The fork can be made by extending
the 8″ rod by 4″, then leaving 2, 2″
prongs spread apart ½″ then sharpening the end on the grinder.

In making the spoon, make the handle 8″
long the same way as the knife, take a thin
piece of rolled steel, cut to shape—
2½″ X 1½″, heat, form with ball
peen hammer. Reheat, and repeat as with knife blade.

Cow Horn Spoon

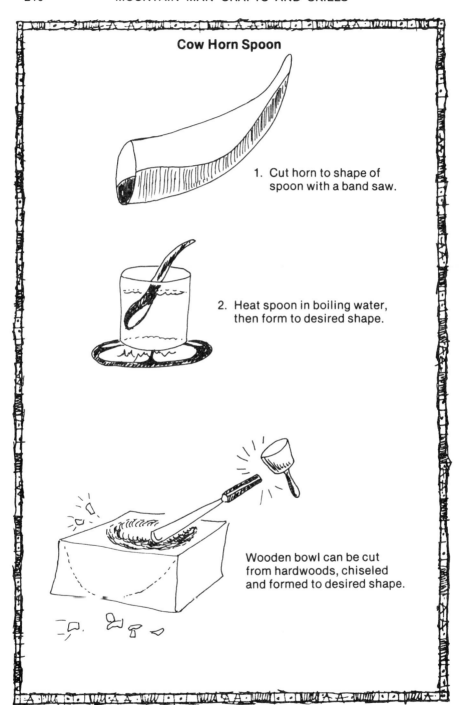

1. Cut horn to shape of spoon with a band saw.

2. Heat spoon in boiling water, then form to desired shape.

Wooden bowl can be cut from hardwoods, chiseled and formed to desired shape.

23

Mountain Man Foods

The food eaten by the trapper and trader of the Fur Trade Era may not please the palate of today's black-powder buff. When times were good, they ate well but when times were bad, reptiles and rodents were a delicacy. When trapping parties went out, hunters were hired specifically to get the food.

1811—the daily ration of the voyager, sometimes called mangeur de lard or "eater of grease" was: 1 qt. of hulled corn, 1 or 2 oz. of suet, tallow or other fat to make something like hominy, and 1 ration of flour which was carried in a handkerchief inside the hat.

1812—Lyed corn, fat pork, cornmeal mush, supplemented with game, turtle, goose and duck eggs, and fowl.

1832—The men received a keg of pork and a bag of flour.

1835—The records at Fort Laramie showed dried buffalo, game, coffee and beans were the mainstay with occasional supplements of flour and a treat of dried apple pie for Christmas Day.

Historical records show that on the trail quite a variety of foods were eaten such as: hard tack, stewed buffalo, badger, beaver, beaver tail, elk, deer, antelope, bear, vultures, fish, panther, dog, and sugar. The parts of the buffalo which were eaten were the flesh along the spine, the tongue, ribs, fat, heart, tenderloins, tepid blood, small intestines and the marrow from the leg bones. These were all wrapped in the green hide for transport. A fat substance the width of a man's hand along the backbone was taken out, dipped in hot grease, and smoked for about 12 hours, then used like bread. The small intestines, called "boudins" were cut in lengths, wrapped around sticks, roasted and then eaten. Marrow, called "trapper's butter," and blood were made into a thick soup. The liver was a great delicacy and was eaten fresh and raw.

Recipes

Jerky: Use about 3 pounds of meat (deer, elk, moose, antelope or beef), cut into strips. Mix the following ingredients and marinate the meat in it overnight covered in the refrigerator.

½	tsp garlic powder	¼	cup soy sauce
½	tsp seasoned salt	¼	cup Worchestershire sauce
1	tsp Accent or MSG	1	tsp onion powder
2	Tbsp liquid smoke	¼	tsp pepper

Lay the marinated strips of meat on an oven rack or on the rack of a dehydrator. Turn the oven on at the very lowest temperature. Crack the oven door open and dry the meat from 8 to 24 hours or until it is chewy.

*Pemmican:*This was an important winter food of the plains tribes and came to be vital to the mountain man. It was nourishing, easily portable and good. Chop dried beef or venison in a blender or grind it between stones if you want to be primitive. Add ½ cup of raisins or other dried fruit per pound of meat and blend them together. Spread this out in a shallow pan and pour melted suet over it, mixing it in. Cool and let it set. Cut it into small sections. It can store for quite a long time.

Pit Oven Roast: Dig a hole 3 feet deep and tightly line it with rocks. Build a good fire in it. When the rocks are thoroughly heated, rake out the fire. Wrap the meat in leaves (or tinfoil), place it in the pit and place some of the rocks on top of it. Cover this with more leaves and earth and let it bake for about two hours.

Fish and Vegetable Stew: Cook wild rice, dried corn and onions together until tender, then add the fish and cook.

Roast Corn: Build a hot fire and let it burn until there is a good bed of coals. Rake the coals away and place green ears of corn in the husks on the hot ground. Cover them with cold ashes and then the hot coals. Build up the fire, and cook for no longer than a half hour.

Hard Tack: Start with a bowl of flour and add water until you can knead the dough without it sticking to your fingers. Roll it out with a rolling pin and cut either in squares or use a bisquit cutter and cut it in rounds. Place them on a cookie sheet and bake them in the oven at 300 degrees and bake until it is hard.

Wild Rice Soup: Wash the rice 3 or 4 times prior to cooking. Use twice as much water as normal for cooking rice. Boil the rice, adding blueberries and sugar to taste.

Corn Bread: Mix the cornmeal with water to form a stiff dough. Add a little salt and make it into a thick cake and bake it in the coals.

Camas Root: Bake in a pit oven and dry for eating.

Squash Pudding: Quarter, pare and boil squash with apples and maple sugar.

Teas, Wintergreen: Cut and dry the leaves or use them fresh. Add 2 spoonfuls of dry leaves per cup of water to boiling water and steep for a few minutes or until it is as strong as you like.

Sassafras Root: Boil root pieces and drink the water.

Edible Plants

There are many books available on edible plants. Only a few of the plants are mentioned here, but a word of caution should be added. Before eating any wild plant, be certain you know exactly what you have; be sure you have the correct plant and not a look alike.

Salad Greens: Many plants can be used for salad such as dandelion leaves, chicory and lamb's quarters. Cattail rootstocks can be eaten raw from fall to early spring.

Cooked Greens: Milkweed shoots 2 inches high in the spring and the tops of stinging nettle can both be cooked by the following method. Boil the cleaned plant in water, changing the water when they are almost done. Cook until tender.

Fruit and Berries: Edible plants include wild strawberry, blackberry, wild grape, hazelnut, pinon nut, prickly pear, and currents.

24

Rendezvous Time

In the vast wilds of the West, the trapper could not go to his neighborhood store and replenish his supplies of powder, traps and food staples. Therefore, some type of system for supplying the men in the wilderness was needed. General Ashley, concerned for the economics of his fur business, set the time of July 1, 1825 and a place on the Green River for a "Rendezvous." The term derives from a French word meaning "come" or "come back." He told the trappers he would bring supplies there and purchase their year's pelts. It turned out to be a successful idea and became an annual event for the next 16 years, each year getting bigger.

For most of the year, the trapper spent his time alone or with one or two companions so the annual Rendezvous became for him a great social occasion. There are books such as *Broken Hand*, about the life of Thomas Fitzpatrick by Hafen, *A Majority of Scoundrels* by Berry, and *Rocky Mountain Rendezvous* by Gowans, that give detailed accounts of the events at various Rendezvous.

Rendezvous Today

Throughout the U.S.A., black powder organizations and clubs sponsor annual rendezvous to commemorate the historic rendezvous of the mountain men. Just to observe what goes on at one of these is an experience, but to be a participant lets you know the fun involved. Rendezvous generally run about three days. There is a tipi village (separate from a tin tipi village), a central campfire, a shooting range and traders row. A Booshway is designated to be in charge and to be responsible for the various things involved in setting up a rendezvous.

To find out where a Rendezvous is held in your area, contact your local Chamber of Commerce or Travel Council. They may also know of existing clubs in your area.

If your group or organization desires to have their own rendezvous, here is a recommendation of how to go about it.

1. Select a site that has enough flat ground for the number of tipis expected and check on the land usage regulations for the area.

2. Make sure good latrine facilities are available. Commercial portable latrines can be rented in most areas.

3. If possible, natural water facilities are desirable, but not necessary, as participants can be told to bring their own water.

4. Check on fire conditions. You may not be able to have fires if fire hazards prevail.

5. Have a shooting range that faces away from camping area.

6. Designate an area for trading and children's games.

7. Have a centralized campfire spot well stocked with wood.

8. Set up a registration table at the entrance to the campsite for purposes of collecting fees, determining prizes, etc.

9. The first day can consist of pistol shoots, rifle shoots, and knife throws, with a campfire in the evening for distribution of prizes and storytelling, or community singing.

10. The second day could have rifle shoots, children's games, ladies' competition, ax throwing, candlelight shoot, campfire, awards, etc.

11. The third day could have rifle and cannon shoots, the mountain man run, grudge matches, and the final campfire where you may wish to elect the next year's booshway.

12. The Booshway should have a clean-up committee to clear the area and put it in its original state. Of course, it is the responsible of the individual camper to clean up after himself.

13. Prizes for the competition can be handled through fees or donations.

14. Not all modern mountain men prefer to compete in the shooting but rather enjoy the trading sessions. One way to destroy a fun time is to go with the idea in mind that you are not going to trade, but want cash only. You'll most likely go home with most of what you brought with you.

Black Powder Shoots

To keep the eye in sharp-shooter shape and give the club or group some inner rivalry, some good planned shoots during the year ought to be planned. Many states have muzzle loader deer hunts which could be a fun opportunity for the group to get together. Some novelty shoots are illustrated in a prior chapter and your creativity can produce new ones by the dozens if you want.

Trading Sessions

Most mountain men and their families have some type of craft they specialize in and these items can come in handy for things you may need or want. It's always fun to get together with their trade goods and barter for what appeals to you. Bead work, pouches, horns, rifles, eating utensils, etc., can be put out on a blanket for display and take it from there.

Clubs

Many large towns and cities have some type of Black Powder Clubs ranging from Revolutionary War Era to Mountain Man to Civil War buffs. Check in your local area to see if a club does exist. If not, and you desire to form one, here are a few suggestions as to how to proceed.

1. Advertise locally that you're interested in forming a club and set up a meeting place, time and date.

2. Present your desires and ideas to the group, select a president, vice-president, and secretary plus maybe a range officer for the shoots.

3. Set up by-laws and dues and a meeting place for monthly meetings.

4. Formulate goals of the club and see if annual rendezvous would be feasible.

5. Designate times and places for shoots and trade sessions as well as planning craft nights.

6. School clubs can also be formed.

7. If you wish, you can become affiliated with the National Rifle Muzzle Loaders Association. For information on this, check with your local sports store. If they don't have information on it, get in touch with the National Rifle Association and they can direct you.

25

Mountain Man Stories

In mountain-man circles, a well told tall tale can earn the respect of even the most grizzled veteran of the woods. Originality and creativity play a big part in the fun. Some of the tales are true and some are not exactly true.

Here are some of each to get you started. These stories can be told around the council fire to the adults or to the family prior to bedtime. Naturally, the most fun is to make up your own stories which involve your family names.

The Grandmas' Bear Hunt

This modern mountain-man tale takes place on the south fork of the Weber River in Utah during a trapping expedition. Dave "Straight Shot" Dalton and Dave "Ramrod" Montgomery had loaded up their trapping gear, tipis, their families and their Mother-in-laws and headed out for beaver country. It took them a while to find just the right ponds with enough room nearby to pitch their tipis. They had finally settled on a little spot and had pitched the two tipis on either side of a little stream which ran into a big beaver pond. There really wasn't too much flat ground so that when they got the tipis pitched they found that the tips of the poles were almost touching. It was late in the evening by the time they were all set up and they decided to leave the grub boxes outside for the night to give them more room inside the tipi for all the people. It wasn't long before even the excited children were snuggled asleep in their sleeping bags.

Unfortunately the grub boxes outside proved to be quite a temptation for all the little night critters found in the woods. The quiet hours of the early morning were broken by loud growling and sniffings and it sounded like all tarnation had broken loose. Straight Shot and Ramrod, in their respective tipis, knew that this was no *little* night critter and covered their heads with their capotes and hoped that this disturbance would not require any action on their parts. Finally, all was quiet and the dawn saw heads poking out of the tipi doors surveying the remains of their grub.

The men were all for packing up and going home because they knew what had feasted there during the night. The two grandmas, from their wisdom and knowledge, knew too but they said, "Look, this here was a grizzly bear and you two big mountain men are afraid to go get the bounder. Rather than pack up and miss this rare chance at a family camp out, we'll take care of the critter for you."

They held a brief conference with each other and, leaving some instructions with their daughters to clean up the camp, they walked back to the trucks and got a big inner tube which they had brought with them in case some of the kiddies wanted to go tubing on the last patches of snow they expected to find. Grandmas are always prepared to entertain kids, you know. This big inner tube had been deflated to be packed, of course, so the Dalton's grandma could just barely fit it into her big apron pocket.

When they got back, they looked to see which way the bear tracks went. They went around back of the tipis and found the tracks heading straight up the mountain. Well, off they went up that mountain right after that old bear. It wasn't long before the Montgomery's grandma flushed a big "grizz" right out of some berry bushes and soon the chase was on. The other grandma, slightly higher up the hill, heard a holler and saw that big toothed, furry critter coming up the slope right behind her friend so she put her toes in second gear and started flying. They huffed and puffed as the fur flew and branches cracked.

At the top of this here hill stood two tall quakies. When she saw this, the Dalton's grandma really let the smoke fly so she could get to the top before the old bear did. She tied the ends of the tube to each tree and started pulling back in the middle. Just about that time the other grandma came into sight leading the bear into position and just in time she ducked behind a bush, and the other grandma gave a holler and that old bear came for her. She let him get real close to her, too, before she let go of that inner tube. Pow!! The tube acted like a giant sling shot and caught that old grizz right in his fat middle and shot him through the air down towards camp. Would you believe this bear came sailing through the air and its front paws caught on those tipi poles which were so close together, flipping the bear over, inside out, pulling him right out of his skin? His carcass dropped right into a large pot of boiling water, which the grandmas had instructed their daughters to prepare. That night the families had bear stew for supper instead of the grub the bear had eaten. They sure enjoyed it, too, sitting on their new bear rug. Thereafter, these two grandmas have been the most sought-after bear hunters in the whole state.

The Couger Bear Hunt

Straight Shot and Ramrod were out "grizz" hunting one day, enjoying the beauty of the forest when out of the bushes jumped this monstrous critter that looked like a cross between a bear and a cougar. Trouble was, it was larger than any bear around and those two intrepid hunters weren't about to shake hands with it, so Ramrod took off for the bushes at high speed and Straight Shot headed up the tallest tree around.

Well, Straight Shot must have looked the tastiest because this here cougar bear decided to chase him and have him for dinner, maybe. About a minute later there was Straight Shot standing on the top most limb of the tree, with that creature jumping almost that high, and he sure looked determined enough that he might just make it. From his precarious vantage point, Straight Shot could see that Ramrod was no where around and he knew he had to get help before Ramrod had time to get back. Worst of all, he could see his rifle just under the feet of that beast. He'd sort of dropped it in the climb. Things were getting quite desperate and help just wasn't coming. There was only one thing to do and that was to take care of the mean feller himself. But how, that was the question.

He sat down on the limb and tried to kick the cougar bear's nose as he jumped. All that did was almost knock him off the limb. He spit in his eye, but that didn't have any affect either. Straight Shot tried his meanest look but that just made the critter laugh. He couldn't climb up any higher, cause he'd plumb run out o' tree. He figured there was only one thing left to do. That was to get brave, and grab his whiskers on the next jump and maybe if he yanked hard enough, that would send him howling. He got set, the cougar bear jumped, but it was a clear miss. It almost caused heart failure. He had no other choice but to try again. This time he could see the beast was all ready for a mighty spring. The varmint jumped. Straight Shot closed his eyes and grabbed for all he was worth.

'Bout this time Ramrod got back, and right before his eyes a spectacle took place that was unbelievable. The cougar bear jumped so high that Straight Shot's arm went right down his gullet. With all his strength he yanked back. What he didn't know, since his eyes were closed, was that he had a hold of that couger bear's tail bone. When he opened his eyes there he was hanging on to an inside out cougar bear skin and one naked cougar bear was yelping through the woods embarrassed as all get out, and one Ramrod flat on his face in total shock.

Well, Straight Shot being the good fellow he is, gave Ramrod the hide which is on his floor to this day and Straight Shot made a necklace of cougar bear claws which someone cordially lifted from him.

Herb The Great Beaver

Ramrod and Straight Shot were out on a trapping expedition with their families and had just finished a fine supper after a hard day of trapping and skinning. The parents and children snuggled down under their blankets for a good nights rest. As always, the parents fell asleep first and the children lay there thinking of the fun they would have the next day. Suddenly at the tipi door came a loud clap, clap, clap. The children peeked from under the blanket only to see what looked like a giant beaver standing at the door. It Was! The kids jumped up and ran to the door to see if it was only a dream. It Wasn't!!

Well, as such things go, this particular beaver happened to talk and as the kids approached him he turned and said, "Hi, I'm Herb, would you like to have some fun with me?" Who could refuse. It was a nice mild moonlit evening, with stars sparkling all over. "Hop on my tail and I'll take you for a ride," and away they went.

Herb took them down his favorite slide which was almost like a roller coaster. The children shrieked with laughter. Next he took them for a ride out onto the pond, being very careful to keep them out of the water. He flipped them up in the air with his tail, then rolled over in the water, shook himself and caught them on his neck. He then challenged them to a log walking contest on some fallen trees. Naturally, being the expert, he won. "Come on," he said, "I'll chow you tho inoido of my lodgc." Off thcy wcnt and to their surprise, there in front of them was a beaver lodge as big as a house. In they went. Inside, on the left was a large closet where the beaver family hung their winter coats, and on the right side was a large grinder the beaver used to sharpen their teeth. There was a living room with a fireplace, a large carved table and chairs, a family painting on the wall, and a toy box just stuffed with carved wooden toys. As they went into the kitchen they saw a big pot on the stove with stewing oak bark with a touch of aspen in it. Sticking out of a big jar were honey dipped willow sticks. They peeked in another room and there were two smaller beaver nestled under the covers of a big carved wooden frame bed.

Well, that reminded them that they themselves were supposed to be in bed and had better be on their way. Herb said, "Hop on my tail and we'll slide all the way to your tipi." So off they went.

Suddenly it was morning and the smell of cooking bacon made the childrens' mouths water. They jumped up to tell their parents of the exciting night they had had. After the parents listened patiently to them they commented that they really had fantastic dreams and enjoyed their story, and the children were sent off to play. There was one thing that was strange though, the parents noticed that all twelve of the children were wearing necklaces with a carved beaver dangling from it.

Jedediah Smith, Trapper and Explorer

Jedediah Smith started his career as a mountain man with the original 100 Ashley men to ascend the Missouri.

While out on a hunt he was attacked by a "grizz." Fortunately his two companions were able to kill the bear after it had only ripped his scalp, torn one ear and crushed several ribs. James Clyman, one of his companions, was asked by Jed to sew him back together and he did.

During this particular trip in 1825 Jed crossed what is now known as the South Pass into Oregon and was one of the first to do so. In 1826 he made his way into California with a trapping party seeking new fields for fur. It was a painful journey, starting with 50 horses and ending up with 18. The territory at this time was under Spanish control and Jed and his men were not welcome. He was asked to leave, which he did, going back through the San Joachim Valley, trapping as they went. He left some of his men by the way. When they had to cross the Nevada-Utah salt flats he thought he might give up the ghost but they survived the ordeal. The party successfully made it to the July Rendezvous.

Jed must have had this insatiable hunger for adventure and self torment because he decided to go back to California. Away he went again to pick up the remainder of his men and again he met with the hostilities of Indians and nature.

By the time he got to California he found that some of his men had engaged in the Spanish conflict which was going on at that time and soon after arriving he found himself on a boat headed for Mexico for a six week stint in jail with his men. After being taken back to California he was told never to appear again in the territory or it would mean certain death.

By November he had returned by way of the Oregon country and arrived at Fort Vancouver with only three men, the rest having been killed by Indians the previous July.

Finally he made his way back and worked as one of the leaders with Jackson and Sublette until he was killed on the Cimarran River by the Comanche at the age of 32.

Hugh Glass
"Almost Bear Meat"

Hugh Glass, hired as a hunter for the Henry party coming out of the Missouri to the Grand, had been around for awhile and was known for his grumpy attitude. He and some other hunters were out in front of the main party hunting for game when Hugh broke through some scrub brush right into the arms of a she-bear with cubs. A welcome sight it wasn't, for before Hugh could do a thing she chomped on his neck, took the flesh and gave it to the cubs, and came back for more. She took a leg and worked him over again. When more of the hunting party broke in and shot at her she temporarily stopped, chased them, and then went back to claw his chest and arms. She was finally brought down with another volley of shots.

Hugh was on his way to the next world they figured and the party waited that afternoon for him to die. Then they could bury him and be on their way. Well, he hung on and the decision was made to have two volunteers stay behind to bury the body and then hightail it out of there since they were in hostile country. These two volunteers were non other than Jim Bridger, quite a youth at the time, and John Fitzgerald.

The next day Henry headed out leaving the three behind. On the way he encountered a group of hostile Mandan and lost two men in the ensuing battle. The rest of the party finally arrived at Henry's fort on the Yellowstone. Bridger and Fitzgerald finally pulled in to report Glass's death. They claimed he lasted five days prior to going under. The group decided to abandon this settlement because of Indian problems and headed for the Bighorn. Fitzgerald had had enough by this time and headed for civilization. He joined the army at Fort Atkinson.

By December Henry had rebuilt Manuel Lisa's old fort on the Bighorn and had sent a small party out to trap the tributaries of the Yellowstone.

While all this was taking place something else was happening which is almost unbelievable. Hugh Glass lay where Bridger and Fitzgerald had left him. He had heard Fitzgerald finally talk Bridger into taking his rifle, knife and possibles and abandoning him to the wolves. With this he swore he'd live to have revenge on these two. After they departed, with what little strength he had left, he pulled himself to a spring, nibbled some wild berries and almost drowned trying to get a sip of water. After ten days of doing this he decided to head out to Fort Kiowa, 100 miles away. He began to crawl, walk and drag himself, finding what he could to eat. The thing that sustained him, besides the dead buffalo and other odd scraps and berries he found, was his strong desire for revenge. After a long period of time he made it to Fort Kiowa, where he fully recovered.

Here he went out with a party under a man by the name of Langevin who was headed for Mandan territory. Right below the Indian village he was put ashore and was surprised and pursued by a war party of Arikara. He barely escaped, with the help of a mounted Mandan. Langevin and his men were all killed. From the Columbia Fur Company post he headed for Henry's old fort, found it abandoned and took off for the Bighorn and Henry's fort.

By New Years Day he reached the fort and there found the first of the two scoundrels who had left him for dead. This was Jim Bridger. As Glass opened the door to the commissary, Bridger, sitting with others looked up to what must have been a horrible shock. There stood an ugly scarred creature of a ghost. Bridger himself must have looked like he'd seen a ghost.

Glass, after taking one long look at Bridger, decided to let him live, saying his youthfulness was to be forgiven but that he would surely avenge himself on Fitzgerald, he being the one that had talked Bridger into leaving.

A few days later Henry needed five men to get a message to Ashley down the Missouri and allowed Glass to be one of them. On the way down the Platte, this party fell into the hands of the Arikara and again Glass escaped with his life.

By June he finally reached Fort Kiowa, and then headed back down the Missouri to Fort Atkinson. Here he met Fitzgerald, and in uniform at that. After sizing up the situation, Glass decided he couldn't destroy government without getting into trouble so he decided "he warn't worth killing no how."

By 1833, he finally met his doom in the mountains by the hands of the Arikara, thus ending the life of one of the great legends.

James P. Beckworth
"Trapper and Chief of the Crows"

A man by the name of Greenwood, who was married to a Crow woman, was always asked by the Crows about a defeat of the Blackfeet at the '28 Rendezvous and decided a good story might pacify them so he told them of the great trapper who had been involved in the battle. He said that this great fighter had been captured from his Indian parents in his youth and raised white. As he told, in a perhaps exaggerated form, the deeds of this man, the Indians became quite impressed and said they would like to purchase this man back from the whites, believing that he was really of Crow parentage. Greenwood said, no deal.

Well, as things would have it, Jim Bridger and James Beckworth were out on a hunting trip. Beckworth departed in a different direction, only to find himself surrounded by a herd of Indian war horses. Having been spotted by the Crow he was taken to the council for "observation." Discovering a mole on his eyelid matched the description of the great trapper and fighter in the story told by Greenwood, Beckworth became an instant chief. He ended up with four young ladies, a wife, twenty horses and gear to go with them. A great feast and celebration took place. Beckworth decided to stay with the Crow and became a great leader among them.

Jim Bridger

Bridger began his trek west with a group of men formed by General Ashley, at the age of 18 and eventually became one of the most famous mountain men. With the gifts of a photographic mind and good common sense he was able to live to the age of 77 and at that time that was a fete in itself.

"Old Gabe" was his mountain name and he was known for being an Indian fighter and a shrewd businessman as well as a great story teller.

One of his trapping expeditions led him down the Bear River and when he came to a great expanse of water he though he had reached the Pacific Ocean, especially after he smacked the salty brine on the water. After further explorations he found himself on a great lake of salt water and is credited with being the first white man to see the Great Salt Lake.

When he saw the writing on the wall with the fur trade going out, he built a fort on what later became part of the Oregon Trail. He married an Indian and was very close to the Shoshone which proved to help him a great deal. He became a trail guide for wagon trains and helped the Mormons locate in the Salt Lake Valley. He also became chief of scouts for the U. S. Army.

Although he could not read, he found Shakespeare to his liking and had his works read to him by a boy. Here was this "Old Gabe" going around quoting Shakespeare to people. He finally died, a blind man, having lived a very eventful life and outliving most of his contemporaries.

26

Glossary

Alumn	Ammonium Sulfate, used for tanning.
Antler	External bone from Deer, Elk, or Moose.
Artificial Sinew	Wax coated nylon used for sewing.
Awl	Pointed horn or metal to punch holes in leather.
Bakers Tent	Canvas lean-to.
Ball Puller	Screw attached to ramrod used to pull a stuck ball out of the barrel.
Bank set	Trap set on the edge of the water.
Beaver	Large fur bearing animal, dam builder and logger. Two distinctive features are the large sharp teeth and flat tail. It lives in most areas of the U.S.
Bit	Blade of an ax.
Black Powder	Explosive mixture of potassium nitrate, charcoal and sulfur.
Block printing Ink	Oil base ink used for scrimshaw.
Booty	Liner for moccasin used in winter.
Borax	Powdered soap used for cleaning hides.
Bow drill	Implement used to start a fire.
Breechcloth	Strip of material used as center section of leggings.
Buckskin	Leather made from a deer hide.
Cap	Used on the nipple of a percussion rifle to ignite the powder.
Capote	Coat made from a blanket.
Cased hide	A hide that is cut only at the back legs then pulled off the animal in a tube.

Charred cloth	Pure cotton cloth cooked in a closed can until it is black.
Conibear Trap	Square, steel spring killer trap.
Dam set	Beaver trap set on a broken spot in the dam.
Dangle	Trinket to hang from fringe on clothes and other articles.
Double Set Trigger	Two triggers on a rifle. One is used to cock the other for a light touch or a hair trigger.
Draw knife	Double handled knife used for fleshing hides.
Draw string	Strings on a pouch to pull it shut.
Dremel	Small hand-held electric drill.
Drowning Stake	Stake put out in the water away from the trap so that the animal will tangle on the stake and drown.
Epoxy	Glue requiring a hardener.
Etching Needle	Hardened steel tipped needle used for scrimshaw.
Eye	The hole in the ax head to set the handle in.
Fire pit	A Pit in the tipi dug to build a fire in and to cook on.
Flash pan	Portion on the lock of a flintlock rifle that holds the powder which catches the sparks.
Flask	Container to carry water, powder or lead balls.
Fleshing	Taking the meat and fat off a hide.
Fleshing beam	Wooden beam to throw the hide over when fleshing.
Flint and steel	High carbon steel and flint which is struck together to create sparks for starting a fire.
Flintlock	A rifle fired by a hammer which holds a flint which strikes the frizzen and ignites the powder.
Forging	Welding steel together with flax.
Fringe	Thin strands of leather on clothing which draws water when the clothing is wet.
Frizzen	Steel leaf used to create a spark on a flint-lock rifle.
Glovers needle	A leather needle with a triangular pointed tip.
Green River Knives	Knives made in the oldest knife factory in the U.S. They were used by the mountain men.
Hardtack	Flour and water biscuit baked hard.
Helve	The handle of an ax.

Hem	Material folded over with raw edge in and sewn down.
Hide	The skin of an animal.
Hydrated lime	Powdered lime used in the dehairing process.
Jaw	Portion of the hammer which holds the flint on a flintlock.
Jerky	Dried, seasoned meat.
Krylon Spray	A clear Acrylic · pray used on horns, etc..
Latrine	Bathroom
Lazy squaw stitch	Sewing three or four beads at a time onto the backing.
Leg trap	A leaf spring trap with a double jaw.
Leggings	Pants without a middle section which requires a breechcloth.
Lock	Portion of a rifle which holds the hammer and spring mechanism.
Log set	Trap set on a log which has been used by by the animal.
Loom	A frame to string beading on.
Moccasins	Leather shoes worn by the Indians and trappers.
Muskrat	Fur bearing animal that lives in marsh and water, found throughout the U.S.
Muslin	A plain woven cotton fabric.
Nipple	Part of a rifle which holds the brass or copper percussion cap which fires the rifle.
Nipple pick	A thin wire used to clear a clogged nipple or touch hole.
Nipple wrench	A socket wrench used to remove the nipple from the rifle.
Non-iodized salt	A table or canning salt lacking iodine used for tanning.
Parfleche	Indian rawhide bag or folded rawhide to carry soft belongings in.
Patch	Pure cotton piece used between powder and ball.
Patch knife	Small sharp knife used to cut patches for black powder shooting.
Pemmican	Dried meat and fruit mixed with suet.
Possibles bag	A bag with a shoulder strap used to carry small belongings and shooting accessories.
Powder horn	Usually a cow horn fitted with plugs on the ends used to carry gun powder.

Powder measure	Device used to measure the grains of powder needed for different caliber rifles.
Primer	Fine grained black powder used in the flash pan of a flintlock.
Primer horn	Small horn used to carry the primer powder for a flintlock.
Pulling Bench	A bench with a sawblade attached used for stretching hides.
Pulling Stake	A pointed stake used for stretching hides.
Quillwork	Decorative work on leather made with porcupine quills.
Ramrod	A long rod used to push the patch and ball down the gun barrel.
Rawhide	The hide of an animal, dehaired, cleaned, stretched and dried.
Relaxed hide	A soft droopy hide, not stiff or dry.
Rendezvous	Annual meeting of the trappers to resupply for the next season.
Rivets	Brass nails that clamp together to hold leather and handles together.
Rosette	The bone at the base of the horn, also a round piece of beadwork.
Sash	A tie belt without a buckle
Scabbard	A covering for a knife or rifle.
Scent mound	Usually a mound of dirt on the waters edge used by muskrat and beaver to leave scent or droppings.
Scrimshaw	A method of engraving on horn or bone.
Seam	The joining of two pieces of material.
Sharpening steel	A tool used for refining the sharpness on a knife.
Shoot	A rifle shooting contest
Short start	A knob with two short dowels to start the patch and ball down the barrel.
Sinew	Tendons of an animal used for sewing.
Skive	To shave the edge of a leather item to make it thinner.
Snow cave	Temporary shelter made of snow.
Snow shoes	A framed webbing made to use in walking on snow.
Sulphonated oil	An oil used in softening hides.
Tanning Solution	Salt and Alumn or other chemicals used to to treat a hide so that it will stretch and soften.

Tassel	Long strip of material hanging from clothes.
Thimble	The round barrel shaped pieces located under the barrel of a rifle which hold the ramrod.
Throwing ax	An ax worn on the belt used for throwing contests as well as for cutting small twigs.
Ties	Cords used to tie tipi and tents to poles and stakes.
Tinder box	Small tin box used to carry charred cloth in.
Tipi	Connical dwelling made of hides or canvas used by the Plains Indians and transported by travois
Tooling	Carving in leather
Touch hole	A hole in the barrel of a rifle which catches the spark from flash pan.
Towsing	To pull and stretch a hide back and forth over a rope.
Trade box	A chest-shaped wooden box used to carry trade goods.
Travois	A wooden frame pulled by a horse with the ends dragging on the ground used to carry belongings.
Tripod	A three legged frame used to hang kettles over the fire.
Vegetable tanned leather	Leather tanner with tannin from oak bark which is stiff and good for tooling, not suitable for garments.
Welt	Extra piece of leather sewn between the two pieces of the garment for reinforcing the seam.
Whet stone	A stone used for sharpening knives.
Willow shair	A backrest made of willow sticks supported by a tripod
Worm	A wire jig attached to the ramrod used to pull patches out of the barrel.

27

Annotated Bibliography of Selected Books

Association, Inc., 1975, 352 pages. Good photography and illustrations of animals throughout the world. Good for reference to do wildlife scrimshaw.

Billington, Ray Allen, *Westward Expansion,* New York, MacMillan Publishing Co., 1974, 805 pages. This is a good history book concerning the trek West, the people involved, the trades, and industry.

Blandford, Percy W., *How to Make Your Own Knives. . . . etc.,* Blue Ridge Summit, Pa., Tah Books, 1979, 252 pages. Illustrated book contains not only knife making but how to make other tools and knife sheaths.

Chausler, Walter S., *Successful Trapping Methods,* New York, Van Nostrand Reinhold Company, 1968, 161 pages. Illustrated book gives fairly good explanations of trapping fur bearing animals, tools to use, and how they are graded.

Cleland, Robert G., *This Reckless Breed of Men,* Albuquerque, University of New Mexico Press, 1976, 361 pages. History of such men as Jed Smith, Joe Walker, and the Sante Fe and Taos trappers. Illustrated with maps.

Dorian, E., and Wilson, W. N., *Trails West and the Men Who Made Them,* New York, McGraw-Hill Book Company Inc., 1955, 89 pages. This small book deals with a few prominent trappers.

Edwards, Edward B., *Pattern and Design with Dynamic Symmetry,* New York, Dover Publications, Inc., 1967. A mathematical approach to designing geometric borders and patterns. Good for ideas on scrimshaw borders.

Finnerty, Edward., *Trappers, Traps, and Trapping,* South Brunswick and New York, A. S. Barnes and Company, 1976. 158 pages. Black and white drawings, gives trapping methods as well as care of pelts, scents, baits, cabin designs, and cabin cooking.

Gilbert, E. W., Lilt, B., *The Exploration of Western America, 1800-1850,* New York, Cooper Squall Publishers, Inc., 1966, 233 pages. A historical account of climate, terrain, animals, Indians, Lewis and Clark, British and American fur trade.

Gowans, Fred R., *Rocky Mountain Rendezvous,* Provo, Utah, Brigham Young University Press, 1977, 310 pages. Maps and photographs of Rendezvous sites as well as the history of each of the rendezvous are contained in this book with excerpts from letters, etc., from some of the original trappers.

Grant, Bruce, *Encyclopedia of Rawhide and Leather Braiding,* Maryland, Cornell Maritime Press, Inc., 1972, 528 pages. Illustrated guide to every conceivable braid there is in rawhide or leather. A very good book to learn how to do it.

Hafen, Leroy R., *The Mountain Men and the Fur Trade of the Far West,* Glendale California, The Arthur H. Clarke Co., 1965 to 1972, 10 volumes at about 400 pages each. These volumes include well researched biographies of close to 300 mountain men and their lives. Compiled by various authors. Also compiles some interesting statistics regarding the group as a whole, their marriages, ages, how long they were in the mountains, and what they did after they left.

Haines, Aubrey L., *Journal of a Trapper 1834-43, Osborne Russell,* University of Nebraska Press, Lincoln, Nebraska, Bison Publishers, 1970, 191 pages. Biography of Osborne Russell and maps of his travels while a trapper in the Rocky Mountains. Very factual.

Hultgren, Ken, *The Art of Animal Drawing,* New York, McGraw-Hill Book Company Inc., 1950, 134 pages. This contains many ink illustrations which serve as excellent patterns for scrimshaw.

Hunt, W. Ben, *The Complete How-To Book of Indian Craft,* London, England, MacMillan Publishers, 1973, 179 pages. One of the best illustrated craft books on Indian skills.

Kauffman, Henry J., *American Axes,* Brattleboro, Vermont, The Stephen Greene Press, 1972, 151 pages. Illustrated history and making of the American ax.

Mails, Thomas E., *The People Called Apache,* Englewood Cliffs, New Jersey, Prentice-Hall, Inc., 1974, 447 pages. A history and excellent drawings of the Apache costumes and crafts.

Mason, Bernard S., *The Book of Indian Crafts and Costumes,* New York, New York, The Ronald Press Company, 1946, 116 pages. Good basic book on Indian crafts.

Mayes, Jim, *How to Make Your Own Knives,* New York, Everest House Publishers, 1978, 191 pages. Contains everything from the history of knives, understanding metals, designing the knife, making it, to where you can order all you need for supplies. Photograph illustrated.

Murie, Olaus J., *The Peterson Field Guide Series, A Field Guide to Animal Tracks,* Boston, Massachusetts, Houghton Mifflin Company, 1974, 356 pages. Good illustrations for learning animal tracks and signs.

O'Connor, Jack, *The Big Game Animals of North America,* New York, Outdoor Life, E. P. Dalton and Co., Inc., 1961, 264 pages. Ink and color illustrations of big game that would be very useful for reference in scrimshaw work.

Olsen, Larry Dean, *Outdoor Survival Skills,* New York, New York, Pocket Book Publishers, 1970, 246 pages. Illustrated book on survival which shows primitive ways of surviving.

Reader's Digest, *"Our Magnificent Wildlife,"* Pleasantville, New York, Montreal, Sydney, The Reader's Digest Association, Inc., 1975, 352 pages. Color photographs and illustrations of animals throughout the world. Good reference for doing wildlife scrimshaw.

Reader's Digest, *Story of the Great American West,* Pleasantville New York, Montreal, The Reader's Digest Association, Inc., 1977, 384 pages. Color illustrated book gives an excellent insight into the opening of the West by various groups. Great selection on the era of the trapper.

Reinfeld, Fred *Trappers of the West,* New York, Thomas Y. Crowell Company, 1957, 153 pages. Easy to read, colorful stories of the Beaver trade, John Colter, Jim Bridger, etc.

Russell, Carl P., *Firearms, Traps, and Tools of the Mountain Men,* Albuquerque, New Mexico, University of New Mexico Press, 1977, 426 pages. Well documented and illustrated book of tools of the mountain men.

Ruxton, George F., *Life in the Far West Among the Indians and Mountain Men 1846-1847,* Glorieta, New Mexico, The Rio Grande Press Inc., 1972, 235 pages. Description of the West, travel, pioneer and frontier life.

Salomon, Julian Harris, *The Book of Indian Crafts and Indian Lore,* New York, New York, Harper and Row Publishers, 1928, 410 pages. Extensive crafts book with more writing than illustrations.

Sandoz, Mari, *The Beaver Men,* Lincoln, Nebraska, London, University of Nebraska Press, 1978, 335 pages. A good history of the fur companies, French, Scottish, and American trappers. It is detailed concerning Indians and the habits of beavers.

Scholz-Peters, Ruth, *Indian Bead Stringing and Weaving,* New York, New York, Sterling Publishing Company, 1974, 63 pages. A very basic book on beading although it contains no rosettes.

Trueblood, Ted, *The Ted Trueblood Hunting Treasury,* New York, David McKay Company, Inc., 1978, 348 pages. Excellent book for the black powder hunter that wants to learn tracking and hunting of wild game. Black and white photography.

Tunis, Edwin, *Colonial Craftsmen and the Beginnings of American Industry,* Cleveland, Ohio and New York, New York, The World Publishing Company, 1965, 154 pages. Illustrated book on the crafts of early America.

Weygers, Alexander G., *The Making of Tools,* New York, Van Nostrand Reinhold Company, 1973, 93 pages. Illustrated book on how to design, sharpen, and temper tools from scrap steel.

Whitford, Andrew H., *North American Indian Arts,* New York, New York, Golden Press, Western Publishing Company, Inc., 1970, 160 pages. This pocket size book has color drawings of Indian crafts throughout the U.S. explaining uses and how the items were made. Very useful.

Wigginton, Eliot, *Foxfire 4,* Garden City, New York, Anchor Press/ Doubleday, 1977, 496 pages. A compilation of crafts by different craftsmen done by high school students in the Appalachian Mountains. It consists of knife making, logging, cheese making, etc. There are three prior books to this one, and they are great for self instruction on basic living skills.

Wigginton, Eliot, *Foxfire 5,* Garden City, New York, Anchor Press/ Doubleday, 1979, 511 pages. This is an exceptional book for the mountain man. It has major sections on ironmaking, blacksmithing, bear hunting, and over 200 pages on black powder gunmaking.

Young, Jean, *Woodstock Craftsman Manuel 2,* New York, Washington, Praeger Publishers, 1973, 288 pages. A general crafts book on items such as stained glass and tipi making.

28

Appendix

Mountain Man Crafts as a Secondary School Course

This book can be considered as a basic guide to a course in mountain man crafts. Many clubs, scout troops and school crafts programs are seeking to learn some of the ways of these men of the wilderness. A suggestion for a class curriculum is offered here to give you an idea of how a class could be handled.

Mountain Man Crafts and Skills

Objective: To learn the basic skills, crafts, and history of the mountain man for enjoyment, knowledge and basic living skills.

Facilities

A. A work area must be arranged where there will be facilities for tanning, electric outlets, and tables to work on plus tools and materials to work with.

B. For classroom situations, it would be best for the instructor to obtain some of the materials prior to class such as willows for chair, bow drills, and snowshoes.

Introduction

A. Refer to the bibliography for some good books concerning the history of the mountain men in depth. These stories and accounts will give the student more insight as to the needs for these skills.

B. If you have your own slides and pictures of these crafts skills and get togethers, show them to your class. (If you do not have pictures you may order a set of slides which contain powder horns, buckskin clothing, tipis, beadwork, rifles, pouches, trap setting, willow chairs, fire making tools, and some grizzly mountain men from the author; David Montgomery, 337 E. Holly Circle, Sandy Utah, 84070). This will give an actual idea of what can be done and whet the appetite.

Sequence of Instruction

A. Instruct all individuals as to what tools and materials will be required throughout the course.

B. Since most courses of instruction begin in the fall it would be a good time to start on the skills of trapping.

C. Fall also brings the big game hunts, so rifle building and Black powder safety should precede the hunt season.

D. Pouches and powder horns are necessary to carry your possibles for the hunts and shoots so this may be next.

E. With the hides available from the hunt and trapping now would be a good time to go into tanning.

F. Next would come the making of some clothing from the leather made.

G. Time for a field trip to a range for a well supervised small shoot and instruction in fire making plus some tall story telling around a fire. If snow is around it may be a good time to build a snow cave to show what can be done for survival.

H. Now the remainder of the course can be refined and arranged as you desire, doing scrimshaw, bone and horn work, beadwork, knife and scabbard making, food preparation and tipi construction.

I. At the conclusion of the course it is fun to have a rendezvous. Here you can trade, win some shoots, or a knife or tomahawk throw, plus have some other contests besides having a good campout in the tipi to see how they function.

Here it may be noted that this course could be taught as an introductory class of from 8 to 10 weeks doing demonstrations only or it could be a full year in depth course. Have Fun!

Index